PURSUED BY A BEAR

Date Due

BRODART, CO.   Cat. No. 23-233   Printed in U.S.A.

PURSUED BY A BEAR

Talks, Monologues and Tales

Daniel David Moses

TORONTO

Ɵ

Exile Editions
2005

First published in Canada in 2005 by
Exile Editions Ltd.
20 Dale Avenue
Toronto, Ontario, M4W 1K4
telephone: 416 485 9468
www.ExileEditions.com

Library and Archives Canada Cataloguing in Publication

Moses, Daniel David, 1952-

    Pursued by a bear : talks, monologues and tales / Daniel David Moses.

ISBN 1-55096-646-4

    1. Canadian drama (English)--Native authors--History and criticism.
2. Native peoples in literature. 3. Theater--Canada--History. I. Title.

PS8576.O747P87 2005   C812.009'897   C2005-906503-6

Design and Composition: Michael P.M. Callaghan
Cover Painting (detail): Blake Debassige
Typesetting: Moons of Jupiter
Printed in Canada: Gauvin Imprimerie

The publisher would like to acknowledge the financial assistance of
The Canada Council for the Arts.

Conseil des Arts   Canada Council
du Canada   for the Arts

Sales Distribution:
McArthur & Company c/o Harper Collins
1995 Markham Road, Toronto, ON M1B 5M8
toll free: 1 800 387 0117   (fax) 1 800 668 5788

*To Lenore who showed me the way
and Colin who keeps me on it.*

Contents

PURSUED BY A BEAR

An Introduction

"Hope this doesn't turn to ice."

We're already driving through the dark at five o'clock in the afternoon, the dark and an icy spattering rain, or at least that's how I'm remembering that moment late in my last visit to Penticton, B.C.

I'd been there again to give readings from my poetry and plays, and to talk with the students about my practice and my life as a writer, the writing students of the En'owkin International School of First Nations Writing.

And now, after a couple of tiring, pleasant days, I'm being taken to the airport, to catch a too small plane and fly through the weather east to Calgary to catch the red-eye flight back to Toronto.

"Your plane might be delayed," my driver mutters.

We'd already left the neon bright commercial and less lit residential sections of town and were passing through a few blocks of warehouses. The night, that an overcast and the month of November and the mountain ranges that define the Okanagan Valley create, was around us like deep water, clear and black. It felt so luxurious in its slick darkness, all I wanted to do was fall asleep, all I wanted was to hibernate a bit once the plane took off from Calgary, if I wasn't going to be able to see the stars.

I'd remembered from earlier trips through the mountains how near and vivid the constellations can appear through the lens of high altitude air, and was feeling disappointed that night by all the clouds.

In the car, by the blue dashboard lights, over the murmuring of the radio's distant news announcer's voice, my driver lady, who I think is a Prairie woman, Cree or Métis, who is one of the writing instructors I've met for the first time these few days, says, "Can I ask? What clan are you?"

The traffic light ahead turns red and we coast to a stop through the wet.

I hesitate.

I think now that I was embarrassed, not wanting to try to explain again that somewhere in the past, in the change over to Christianity, my family mostly lost track of or chose not to preserve traditional knowledge.

I was not wanting to admit in that moment, after spending the last couple of days being a professional First Nations writer role model for the students, that I occasionally feel like an Indian in law only.

Those occasions are usually the ones where I'm faced with questions that assume on my part a certain knowledge of the collective past; a rather romantic assumption that doesn't seem to take into account the hundreds of years of contact and acculturation and accommodation that make up that past, in the eastern parts of Canada at least. Those questions mostly come from white people.

Do you speak your native language? Do you have an Indian name? What's your clan?

There in the west where the coming of the white man is almost yet within living memory, I hesitated.

I was too tired to want to and didn't really have time to tell my driver the story of how my mother for years understood that her own mother and therefore she, herself, as the oldest girl would, in the old world, have been a clan mother. The clan mother was the woman our people entrusted with the job of picking the man, of "putting horns on him," who would act as our leader, our chief. She was also the one who could "de-horn" a bad leader.

My mother had gathered somehow that we were turtle clan people and made a persistent effort to celebrate that allegiance. I'm sure there accumulated in our house dozens of knickknack turtles, ceramic and wood, metal and mineral, beaded and woven, lining windowpanes and sills, decorating end tables and book shelves, before an older relative, probably my grandmother's half-sister, corrected her.

And of course the kid in me, the kid I was when all that happened, was much happier being related to bears. And the writer I am is pleased that on occasion bears are good enough spirits to make appearances in literature — for instance, that famous stage direction from *The Winter's Tale* — EXIT, PURSUED BY A BEAR — really gave me a frisson the first time I read it, still gives me something to hang onto. And of course bears making fleeting appearances — I don't seem to know them well enough just yet — in my own work. But it does all seem at moments so much romance, literary and relic, so much of that other world, the lost one of my youth or the past.

The driver lady turns the radio down.

I take refuge in a small-talk tone. "Oh, our family, we're supposed to be bear clan."

The light changes, my driver steers into a right-hand turn. She catches my eye and nods. "That's what I thought."

I frown but in the dark she can't see. "What do you mean?"

"Oh, you know. The way you act. The way you came into that party last night."

"The way I came into the party?"

"You kinda just stopped in the doorway and lurked there for a second or two."

"I 'lurked'? Sorry."

"No, that's how bears act coming into a new territory. They check it out before they make their move."

We're pulling up in front of the terminal.

"I think I was just looking for the beer."

"No, no, you went for the Nanaimo bars first. Definitely bear."

We laugh.

I jump out of the car and grab my book bag and suitcase from the back seat.

I thank her again for her help in getting me around to my appearances.

"Good luck," she says, looking again at the rain. She waves and drives off into the dark.

I check in and the woman at the desk assures me the rain isn't freezing and there won't be any delay getting out.

As I wait for the flight to be called and remember what my driver lady said about bears, there in that mountain town, even in that brightly lit lounge, they seem very present.

Maybe I will be able to hibernate after all on the long flight through the star-rich night back to T.O.

(2005)

SPOOKY

An Essay

"Spooky"?

Yes. That's the word.

Spooky.

It was last year, May, and we were rehearsing my play, *Coyote City*, soon to open at the Native Canadian Centre of Toronto. And it must have been a Tuesday well into the rehearsal period, a first day back at work after our Sunday and Monday off. And one of the actresses came to me and told me that over the weekend she had gone home to the reserve and to Longhouse and that afterwards she had had a vision and that it was because of my play.

Rings of fire burning dry fields of grain is the image I remember, but I could be mistaken. I wasn't giving her vision my entire attention. Part of my mind was already at the table inside the rehearsal hall, wondering how we would get the car and bus scene to work. Another was focusing on my actress' face, on her wide and beautiful eyes, her excitement. And one part of me was standing still, thrilled and pleased to be privy to these personal experiences of the supernatural.

Which, of course, meant that one further part of my mind was in panic, retreat, covering its ears, not wanting any more of this spooky stuff. My actress' story was only the most recent in a series of spiritual experiences that the more traditionally minded members of my cast and crew had been bringing into rehearsal, bringing that energy to the play and, of course, to me.

Coyote City can be described most simply as a ghost story. It's structured as a journey and a chase from a reserve into a city. Its impetus is the love Lena, a young woman, has for a young man she doesn't know is dead. The play begins with a monologue from the young man, the character Johnny, whom we, the audience, only later discover is already a ghost.

In developing the story for the play, the subtext, the world that the words should imply from the stage or the page, I was surprised to find that I was afraid to make that simple decision. My progress came to a halt as I tried to develop a psychological explanation, tried to say that the character was a figment of Lena's imagination, that she was mad. In my fear, I had stumbled into Romantic cliché and it was getting me nowhere.

Why was I afraid to decide that the ghost was as much a character as the rest? My intuition told me I had to make that proverbial imaginative leap if the play was to work. I had to believe in the ghost as much as I did in the girl or her mother if I was to do justice to the story, the play and the audience.

I have seen girls. I have seen mothers. I have a mother. They're part of my existence and easy to believe in. But I have never seen a ghost. And I don't mean a ghost like my character Johnny or Casper or like in *Ghostbusters* or The Holy Ghost. And I don't mean, at least at this point in my story, a ghost in a dream. I mean wide-awake experience of a spirit, what those so-called scientists working at the fringes of our knowledge have labelled paranormal.

I grew up on a farm on the Six Nations lands along the Grand River near Brantford in southern Ontario. I grew up nominally Anglican in a community of various Christian sects and of the Longhouse, the Iroquoian traditional religious and political system. These form the largely unarticulated base of my understanding of the world.

I grew up on occasion hearing ghost stories rooted in that community, stories I only paid small attention to, because I was being educated to have — let's call it — a western mind, to balance being a good Judaeo-Christian with being scientific. Ghost stories may be thrilling and amusing, art may be thrilling and amusing and sometimes prestigious, but we only really believe in what we can see with our own eyes and measure with our own hands.

How could I possibly believe in a character, write a character who was a ghost? We're advised to write about what we know and at that point I was quite sure I didn't know anyone who was, well, dead.

What I did at the time was sidestep the existential issue. I had to have the ghost character or the play would be dead. That I knew. What I did was try to use my so-called western mind. I argued with myself: Art is, after all, artificial and not a question of believing but of doing. So go ahead and do the ghost. Construct it. What's metaphor for, after all? This death stuff is only symbolic. Come on, you coward. It's only a story, only words.

Only words.

My ghost character Johnny did come alive eventually, when I started to treat his deadness as ordinary, which, of course, despite pomp and circumstance, it is. Everyone has problems, especially in drama, and Johnny's was that he simply didn't know that he no longer belonged in the material world. I came to believe in Johnny, as I had to, since the concerns of the play *Coyote City* are the conflict between the material and the spiritual, and Johnny, as a ghost, focused that conflict.

The play progressed, although I still had to deal in as forthright a manner as I could with this epistemological prejudice when I workshopped the piece. I had to steer my director away from psychological explanations of the ghost, warning her that it would oversimplify parts of the play and make the rest of it absurd. Johnny's a real ghost, I insisted, feeling, despite my intuition, oxymoronic even as I said it. Okay, my director replied deliberately. I admit that she came with me as far as she could, though I did have to put up with ironic renditions of the theme music from *The Twilight Zone* the first few times we came to work on any scene with the ghost.

As a balance to this and a support to my intuition were the Native performers in the cast, who had no trouble at all accepting that one character was a ghost. The idea was as familiar to them as the sun.

(A parallel example is a story I heard about one production of the Linda Griffiths/Maria Campbell play *Jessica* which presents a number of animal spirits as characters. It took some extra doing for the non-Native actors to enter into, to believe in the Bear, the Unicorn characters. Meanwhile, the Native actors simply assumed them, second nature.)

Why did I remember the idea of spirits so vaguely?

My years at York and UBC had taught me many things about the techniques of writing. But I had also absorbed a number of what I now see as prejudices about the nature of literature. The trepidation I felt about the haunting of my play *Coyote City* is indicative of the sort of contemporary literary ideas that got stuck in my student head. I'm sure part of me wanted to be too hip to tell anything as old fashioned as a ghost story. University was when I stopped reading science fiction, which had been a staple of my reading life since my teens. Suddenly, it was obviously too popular, too accessible, too far-out to be good literature. Instead, I read the modern, the near postmoderns and, of course, Canadians, who were pointed out to me as examples of the literary ideal. And I was often moved by the beauty and imagination of the writing and in awe of its obvious intelligence and its superb technique. And I felt stretched, educated, edified. I knew what was going on inside those proverbial ivory towers, me, a farm-raised Indian boy. I was dizzy. I tried to learn the lessons these writers offered me.

I tried.

I had a crisis of literary faith and, like most such crises, it hinged upon an almost absurd distinction. I got into a knot over the difference between the real and the true. I thought that good writing should be true and my western mind told me that the real world of facts was true. My poetry collapsed into bare description, looked like documentary haiku, if you can imagine, but without the tradition to inform it. I know I suspected the work was inaccessible, but I didn't know why or how to make it less so. And since I work so intuitively, largely inarticulate, there was no way I knew to ask for help, and no one had the sense to help me. And, as I look back now, I doubt I knew I needed help. I had probably convinced myself I was writing the way I ought to, the way I had been taught to, as I understood it.

I saw a film called *Fake*, a seeming documentary, directed by Orson Welles, about a forger of great works of art. It was also about the ideas of truth and reality and art and, as I remember it now, quoted Picasso declaring that "Art is not Truth: it is the lie that reminds you of the Truth." This idea also stuck in my student head. Suddenly I knew, or was reminded, that literature, art, wasn't about being factual, material (despite the tales I'd heard from my American friends about *The New Yorker*'s meticulous fact checkers), but about spiritual truths, ideals and ideas. Even the film itself, I realized, might really be a fake documentary. I was thrilled. What a playful, tricky guy this Welles was. Writing was suddenly fun again, as far as it went.

As far as it went when I finally got out of university was lyric poetry. Despite the fact that I had studied many genres of writing — plays, poetry, fiction and non-fiction prose (apparently the latter is now called creative documentary), screenplays, essays — I felt (and now believe I was wise to feel) that lyric poetry was the only form in which I could combine the techniques of writing with the only thing I could claim to know as truth, my own experience. I told myself in poetry would I perfect my technique while I gave myself time to grow up. I documented my life in poems about my family, the countryside, those particular lives and deaths. As far as this went, it was good. I had a definite and clear voice. Where it did not go, what it did not express, except, of course, obliquely, was some sense of my understanding of the wider world, the world of ideas and ideals, history, culture, a world I was facing daily.

Working at last independently, with no institutionalized threat of failure and no constant contact with current academic and literary fashions, I began to work haltingly toward a way of writing that could express more of what I felt.

My first choice, a choice I had already made intuitively and only now really articulated to myself, was technical. Taking as my guide the numerous traditional Native cultures that revere dreams as a way of understanding the world, I tried to make poems of dreams, or to incorporate dream images or to just create dreamlike feelings in poems. I started out thinking of this practice as surrealism, but the results, at best, were more like stories or rituals. I stopped naming and just kept doing.

One unexpected bonus of this half-understood aesthetic practice was poetry of irony and humour. Other results were dramatic monologues, implied dialogues, the half-heard discussions of several voices. This was exciting and intriguing.

Now a friend helped me see where I'd arrived on my journey to and from the ivory towers.

I had been part of a workshop for Native writers that started out in a room at the Native Canadian Centre of Toronto and ended up in the living room of one of the other participants, Lenore Keeshig-Tobias. Lenore had done university, consciously looking for ways to write about being a Native person. While I was off, wandering among a confusion of contemporary styles and English

courses, she had been studying storytelling, folklore and presentation. While I was being awed, moved and, more often than
not, dispirited by the great works of contemporary literature, she
was being encouraged by Native literatures. Seeing her recite one
poem to a rapt audience crowded into the Trojan Horse coffee
house on Danforth Avenue, a poem by "Mohawk Poetess" E.
Pauline Johnson, reconfirmed my taste for the oral. (It was perhaps an original taste since Johnson had been the one poet I had
heard talked of beyond the schoolyards of my childhood.)

In our workshop sessions, Lenore reminded me of my own
knowledge of the extent of Native literature. I had been lucky
enough, as a reasonably articulate young Indian man, to land a
summer job back when I was attending university, with the Education Branch of the Department of Indian Affairs in Ottawa.
We were compiling an annotated bibliography of books by or
about Indians. Over three summers, I read and wrote a short re-
view of, on average, a book a day. By the time I left the post I felt
over-full with information about the sad history of my own people.
The picture of honourable people being lied to, cheated, mur-
dered, and finally despised and ignored is neither human nor
pretty. Maybe that's why I retreated into the technical concerns
of a graduate student.

One of the staples of our workshop circle was the sharing of
recent literary discoveries, from both the Native and non-Native
worlds. We would talk about poems, rituals, songs, stories, novels.
We would talk about techniques, always emphasizing the oral.

Among the stories we began paying more attention to were
cycles of stories called Trickster tales. "Trickster" is the generic
name anthropologists have given to a type of character who
shows up in the tales of most of the world's oral literatures.
People experiencing these tales as parts of their everyday life are
not so consciously aware of that essential part of the character's
nature. They know him or, in some cultures, her, by name, names

like Raven, Nanabozo, Weesageechak, Old Man or Coyote. They know the Trickster is a figure of great contradictions, an every man or woman or animal and a nobody in one body, a hero who is also a fool, a fool who is heroic too. They know that if they listen to the stories about the Trickster, they will be entertained while being both instructed and admonished. Being didactic is an honoured function of these tales. They embody concepts about the nature of being human, about the humanity of nature. They deal with the details of oversized pride, great stinking farts, insatiable lust or hunger, and happy accidents. They may tell us how light was brought to humankind or why the anus is wrinkled. They are about the errors of our ways. They deal in extreme situations to comment on and warn about the dilemmas of ordinary ones.

The Trickster is not absent from contemporary Western culture. He shows up with some regularity in the less respected genres like fantasy, musical and science fiction, though usually in forms that show only one of his aspects — often the nastier side, like the Joker in *Batman*, the Master of Ceremonies in *Cabaret*, Bugs Bunny, Peer Gynt.

The good versus evil dichotomy that frames our understanding of the world in contemporary culture cannot, with ease, accept a figure of contradictions and, so, relegates such literary characters to the fringes of our respect with the clowns, the devils and the Indians.

In the animistic understanding of reality that traditionally characterized Native cultures, the extremes of the Trickster are an accepted part of his artificiality, and the contradictions, evidence of his humanity. He is capable of doing good and evil and like any such person should be approached with caution, with suspicious respect.

Mainstream society presents us with heroes, role models, whose strengths we are encouraged to emulate. When a hero shows weakness and fails (remember Ben Johnson?), the entire society fails and is dispirited and we are forced to wallow in the failure. This is identified in literary circles as tragic catharsis, and the best thing about it is we feel so much better when it stops. Native societies present us with Tricksters, examples of behaviour it would do us good not to follow. When a Trickster shows weakness and fails (an example will follow), we are together opened, often in laughter, and reminded of our own humanity. Our laughter is not untouched by sadness, but the experience is more sweet than sour, more encouraging than not.

To me, this seems a better way to create literature, to write in a world that for my entire lifetime has been under threat of more or less instantaneous destruction from atomic weapons and stays under the threat of corruption and extinction by the detritus of the neurotically materialistic ways we live here in the western world.

I want to encourage people. In writing workshops, in everyday life, I meet people who have been spiritually, often physically wounded by the life they live in this society. They hesitate to act for fear of failure, for fear of appearing the fool. "You Can't Beat City Hall" would be their banner, if they were confident enough to organize. The useful thing about the Trickster is that he or she is easily a far greater fool than any of us can ever fear to be, and yet s/he gets up and goes onto further foolishness and/or creativity. Certainly we Native people in our particular historical bind can use this sort of encouragement. Our sense of humour has certainly got us this far. And we are not the only ones who need it.

I see, as you can see, a lot of potential in the Trickster, not simply because of the clarity s/he gives to my life, my view of the world. Although I didn't recognize it at the time, the Trickster was there too in *Coyote City* for me as the writer, the artist.

I went to a performance by Native Earth Performing Arts of a project called The Trickster's Cabaret. (Native Earth is one of the few all-Native theatre companies in the country.) I was acquainted with some of the performers through my work with the Association for Native Development in the Performing and Visual Arts (AND-PVA) and was curious to see how good they were. The piece was a series of monologues and dialogues, as I recall, some original material, some not. Shakespeare, I'm sure, got a going-over. I came out more than impressed. Now, I thought, we've got the actors. They're more than ready. Now, I can start writing that play.

Some months later Lenore showed me a version of a Trickster story, a Coyote story from the Nez Perce people, a lovely story called "Coyote and the Shadow People." As these stories go, it was less raucous, less earthy than usual, but then again its subject matter, the inevitability of death, made it so. Coyote, in profound mourning for his late wife, is allowed by a spirit guide to visit her in the afterlife. The spirit pities Coyote and gives him the opportunity to bring her back to this life. He must not touch her until she has become flesh again. Coyote's love, his lust, overcomes him and he makes his error. He embraces his wife and she is lost to him forever. Later, I would reflect on the parallels and differences between this tale and that of Orpheus and Eurydice (being particularly intrigued by the importance of touch in the Nez Perce story and of sight in the Greek myth), but what I knew immediately was that here I had an inspiration around which I could eventually create a play. I began to make notes. I began writing my play, mixing the story of Coyote and the Shadow People with a more contemporary but parallel story (the play takes place yesterday) of Native people coming into the city, impelled by a phone call from a dead man (an image impressed upon me by seeing an entire volume in an occult bookstore given over to accounts of Phone Calls from the Dead).

Part of the pleasure I felt when I began writing the piece was the thrill of ignoring my own western common sense that said that phone calls from the dead were silly and that no audience in its right mind would put up with the play. Another part of that initial pleasure was the unshakable conviction that a phone call from a dead man was precisely the right image needed to connect, literally and metaphorically, the spiritual and material worlds.

Why did I need to believe in that ghost? I have never seen, as I said, a ghost. But being the author of a ghost story play gives me the appearance of a believer, a co-conspirator, and even non-Native friends opened up to me about experiences with ghosts and other spiritual creatures, stories the waking world hears with grudging indulgence. I hear these tales, I realize, with a hungry excitement. I get spooked.

In a world where Native people, Native traditions assume the existence of a spirit world as a given, a gift, and where non-Native people scoff or keep secrets, I found I could not reject this anecdotal evidence. I had been taught to respect and include other people and their experience in my world. This evidence is, at least, my bread and butter and, in its purest form, my subject matter. (My next piece, a one-act called *The Dreaming Beauty* which takes themes from *Sleeping Beauty* into a Native world view, also had a ghost appear among its characters during composition.) So I admit my own limitations. Just call me spiritually blind and allow me the freedom to fumble in my own time toward meaning in this life.

Let me try to be less ironic, more straightforward. Part of my mind, still inexperienced with the supernatural (though friends promise me eventual, non-sectarian revelation), refuses to believe in a spirit world. This part of my mind uses the psychological and social explanations. If you believe ghosts exist, if your culture tells you they do, they will for you. This part of my mind also admits the attraction of ghosts, the meaning their existence would give the world, and takes this meaning to be the importance of ghosts and of the supernatural in life and literature.

My faith as a writer is the words I work with. What I create from them I always see with a mixture of satisfaction and criticism, recognition and disbelief. What we collectively believe in, what we think the spirit, the meaning of our so-called civilization is, is embodied in our culture, in the worlds and characters of our stories, even if we today, even artists, are encouraged not to believe this, to be inarticulate, uncritical, to call art low or mere entertainment. A ghost is a disembodied spirit; my ghost Johnny was the embodiment of certain values, certain emotions I saw leading toward death. He was a Trickster for me, showing me the limits of my understanding and my spirit, and in the process, I hope, helping both grow into life.

(1989)

THREE SISTERS

A Story about Writing and/or Telling

When I was growing up on a farm on the Six Nations lands on the Grand River in southern Ontario — we called the place "the Reserve" — we were all Indians, those of us who were Christians, and none of us were writers.

Now that I am no longer quite so young and have begun in these last few years to travel there and here to give readings of my plays and poems, to give talks like this one, to appear as a "writer," to actually "career" as a writer — and it does sound like a verb, doesn't it? — all activities which often seem beside the point of the work of writing itself, I have also begun wondering how I got all the way here from my home.

I think that three women have had something to do with it, women I think of as my Three Sisters. Now I'm not related to any of them, and I really know only one of them, but I think I like to think of them this way because it makes at least this one thread of the story of my life in art a bit more familiar.

Familiar.

I guess I should say that this Three Sisters' image comes to me out of Iroquoian lore into the here and now as a metaphor, a literary symbol of a traditional agricultural practice. We used to always plant corn, beans and squash in one hill. The corn supported the vines, the beans put nitrogen into the soil, and the squash kept the insects off. That's the way our Three Sisters helped each other and grew and grew up together, in order to feed us.

So those Three Sisters, my Three Sisters, are not Chekhov's.

What, after all, did we have to do with words at home? Hardly any-thing. We skimmed the local newspaper, went through the mail. We had a radio on whenever we were in the house or the barn — I remember doing the evening milking to the music of Glen Miller. That's where our information came from. And eventually from tel-evision. There were stories eventually on television. I admit that. Tonto, Jay Silverheels, came from our reserve, although his fam-ily, the Smiths, knew him as Harry.

But really, who had time or reason to read?

When my mother went to work away in town as an RNA, a Registered Nurse's Aid, she started to read romance novels, Harle-quins. That's what nurses read.

And my sister turned into an athlete.

And my father, since he's retired, reads Farley Mowat and James Herriot.

But there'd never been either serious reading or storytelling in that house till I came along. So I had neither your liberal edu-cation nor your aboriginal upbringing.

Outside that house, in high school by then, the writers we heard about were not Indians either. Most were English — men, long dead ones. I'm sure there must have been a few Americans too, and probably Canadians, all of them also long gone. None of the work of these writers we studied, young Indians with the stick of examinations over our heads, with the carrot of Christmas, Easter and summer holiday vacations in front of our noses, ever stayed with me unless that work had to be memorized.

> In Xanadu did Kubla Khan
> A stately pleasure dome decree:
> Where Alph, the sacred river, ran
> Through caverns measureless to man
>   Down to a sunless sea.

As much as I hated it at the time, now, it still echoes, memory work. And only since I've studied those poems for my own pleasure has their echo grown profound, a sound not only between the ears but also in the body, through the mouth and lungs, the heart, and sometimes even the fingers and toes. I'm talking beyond prose and through metaphor to something more whole. The poem in the body, of the body, means something to me. That's the sort of poetry, the sounding kind, the kind that most easily fits into memory that I like, that has always drawn me. And perhaps this love for the body of language was first opened up by the liturgy and hymns of that Anglican mission church I was carted to as a kid. The King James Version of the Bible, a language of goodness, the comforts and complexities of ceremony, they give a feeling of a narrative, concrete and necessary, the important story. A civilized or at least Christian way of telling a story, some might say.

And one way of describing what I've so far seen as my job as a writer would be the finding of that narrative, that form, that force, that through-line. And I usually do have to sound it out. That's how I make sense or senses of it. I have to feel it, heart, lungs, et cetera. Whatever idea I have — and I often start with just an idea in my head — I have to work, to write, until the idea can be said by the body entire. I write words that are meant to be spoken and heard, that mean what they must in the air.

And although, of course, I use the stuff, I have come to distrust paper, the way words become abstract, ideal, unconnected, not actual, powerless but precise on the page. I think I think that words whose lair is paper are more likely to be liars. I think I think that truth will out when one utters. I think I trust the told word is true. Or at least that some of you, some of us, will spot what's false. It's so much easier to fool the solitary reader for whom words are written on the page. Alone with a book full of words, who will protect you from their spell? But isn't that thrill of the deluded imagination, the distracted consciousness, what the solitary pleasure of a good read is all about?

The young Indian student I was would have agreed with that. I ate up fat volumes of adventure and science fiction, the Edgars, Rice Burroughs and Allen Poe, Arthur Conan Doyle, A.A. Milne, Tarzan, horrors, Sherlock Holmes and Winnie the Pooh — but nothing you would recognize as poetry or drama. I didn't know Poe wrote poetry then. And except for Poe, I don't now really know or care much about who those writers were. But Poe had his Raven, and, well, us Indians have stories about Ravens.

Inside my parents' house, inside and outside of school, there was one poet we did know about, did hear talk of. E. Pauline Johnson, *Tekahionwake*, had lived just down the Grand River, a drift by canoe of ten minutes or so. And although she had been neither English nor a man, she had written, poetry and stories, and her memory at least was still alive among us, thanks to more memory work:

> *West wind, blow from your prairie nest,*
> *Blow from the mountains, blow from the west*
> *The sail is idle, the sailor too.*
> *O! wind of the west, we wait for you.*

Her memory was still alive among us, thanks also to the old house called "Chiefswood," the mansion that had been her family home and now was a slightly run-down museum. My sister went to work there as a guide one summer, telling visitors — and me — about Emily Pauline, her English mother, her Mohawk father, her sister, about her Mohawk name *Tekahionwake* which means "double Wampum," about the house itself which had front doors on two opposite sides — one to welcome Indian visitors from their canoes on the river, the other for white travellers from carriages and horseback on the roadway. E. Pauline Johnson had become a poet and performer, a celebrity known across our country and in Victorian England as the Mohawk princess — whatever that is — and her sister, who had not approved of her unladylike career or, it was rumoured, her lovers, had become a ghost who was still there, rearranging the desk set, rocking the chair in the drawing room. And the name E. Pauline Johnson was still in evidence, in print and stone. Her poems were and are still in print, and there are memorials and high schools named for her in the city of Brantford and — who knows? — perhaps across the country . . .

You see, I think of her now with some sentiment, as do many of the Native writers I know. Our Foremother, I've called her. Though her literary reputation in the rest of Canada — she used to be on every syllabus — has faded of late, for she wrote as women of her day did, of family and love and country and racism, for she wrote with compelling musicality (not a quality English-speaking Canadians are comfortable with), we hold the fact of her life as an Indian who wrote in our hopes for ourselves, our families, our peoples. That's now.

Then, despite the facts of her life and work, I had no idea that I too might become a writer. I don't think I was a particularly thick-headed young man. I think it still seemed to me to be part of the necessary definition of a writer that one be dead. And there are some sacrifices I still won't make for my art.

It was not till sometime about the middle of high school that I discovered evidence that a writer might be a living creature. It was the late sixties then, and a wave of Canadian nationalism had so soaked into our curriculum that we found ourselves studying living Canadians along with the established dead Americans and Brits. Contemporary writers included the likes of Irving Layton and Leonard Cohen. They had become academic by then.

I found myself attracted to the work of Gwendolyn MacEwen. I still remember the leaf-green cover of her book *The Shadow*

Maker on the poetry shelf in the school library. I liked her use of what seemed ordinary language. I liked the way it could suddenly be musical, rhymes and rhythms. I liked its playfulness, its imagination, the way it changed things. And when her next book, *The Armies of the Moon*, came into the library, its cover silver and navy blue, it seems to me I made a connection, that I discovered that this was the work of a living writer. I'm sure that this discovery was but one of many reasons I made the decision, somewhere in the back of my head, unarticulated but steadfast, that I, too, would at last become a writer.

I strategized my way through two universities, York and UBC, and into two degrees to do it, ended up a bit overloaded by ideas about being a writer. Had tons of technique, but felt a bit hobbled by my own tastes when most my peers were writing stuff that was imagistic, intellectual, interior, self-examining, with a music so subdued and subtle, I was often deaf to it. To me, it all read — in my more unhappy moments — like inferior translations of deservedly obscure foreign poets. And these kids were writing here in Canada.

I wanted poetry to sing, to dance, and the first chance I got, as soon as I'd finished what I thought were the requirements for my degree, my first book — all these lyrical poems — started coming out of me. For example, "March":

> *The light is rain*
> *grey this morning, my breath*
> *fog and the hills dry*
>
> *moss rising through soiled*
> *remnants of snow. Over*
> *night the white at the bottom of*

the lawn has become translucent to
the darkness seeping water is and sap
has threaded red and pliant

yellow back into the pricks and
forks of thickets. The trees shift
their limbs, creaking and forgetting ice

coats and crusty stars. They're getting
ready to bare
their tender tips.

It took what was left of the seventies and some luck, including an introduction via a chance phone call at a writing workshop's closing party, but the poet, and then publisher, bill bissett and his blewointmentpress brought my *Delicate Bodies* out as soon as I was ready in 1980. I had by then moved to the city of Toronto and was working only to buy myself time to write. I attended readings by other writers, was volunteering with the Association for Native Development in the Performing and Visual Arts and working with a circle of other Native people interested in writing.

I had been invited into the group by Lenore Keeshig-Tobias. She's an Anishnabe Kwe, a member of the Chippewas of the Nawash band from the Bruce Peninsula on Georgian Bay, and she had also strategized her way through university, three infant daughters tagging behind, her mind also set on being a writer, but definitely a Native one. She'd read everything she could get her hands on ever written by a Native person or on a Native subject — a hard search then. And she also liked Pauline Johnson, and wasn't afraid to say so.

I mean I was afraid to say so — all those ideas I'd picked up in university.

Now the idea that one might like musicality in poetry was understandable if somehow a bit, well, retrograde — but the idea that one might also like, oh, stanzas, structure, narrative — what perversity!

But Lenore longed for narrative — Lenore who, of course, also knew about Poe and his Raven — particularly narrative with Native content, and as she read she came to see that Native narrative, the tradition of oral storytelling, was where we ought to be.

In the more than a decade that I've known her now, I've seen Lenore transform from a writer of poems and children's stories (an understandable preoccupation if you recall those three daughters, now all for only a short time more teenagers) through the application of writing and presenting techniques, and with the help of a spirit guide — a medicine woman conducted her through a fast — into a storyteller, a playwright, an essayist, a Native literature activist whose questions about cultural theft have upset more than a few smug writers who claim imperiously that stories belong to everybody — even though most stories just won't go from one culture to another without major interpretation. Oh, they claim the imagination is free, like the best things in life, pay no money.

In Native cultures, you see, one can own a story. One can be given or even buy one and then retell it, but it would be immoral at most, or ill-mannered at least, to steal it, to use it without permission, especially since stories have meaning, spirit. Aboriginal copyright, might one say? But add to that a moral and spiritual dimension because it also has to do with individual or collective identity. He who steals my images, my story, steals my soul.

And suddenly I remember that of all the clever things that T.S. Eliot ever wrote, the one repeated quote, I heard it year in, year out, one of those ideas I got in university, was "A good writer borrows, a great writer steals." So did old Eliot then, growing older in England, admit thereby that the best of modernity was based in aesthetic immorality? Was he always so morose, meditating perhaps on theft and the empire?

It seems to me one thing to use and abuse those stories we are all expected, all educated to know something about, expected to own, whether we want to or not — the Bible, Shakespeare, *Don Quixote*, the ancient Romans and Greeks, the Americans (almost all the imperial cultures) — and quite another to appropriate and inevitably misuse the stories of those who own little else in this world. The materialist virtue of greed becomes, in the context of a contest over spiritual property, clearly the sin of genocide.

The intensity of the emotions raised in defence of imaginative freedom against the protests of those of us who are economically and politically powerless looks irrational, looks to me like scapegoating, when there are real economic, political and bureaucratic threats to freedom of speech in Canada.

And the intensity and the irrationality of the reflex accusations of "political correctness" frightens me, makes me suspect those formerly smug writers know exactly what they're doing to us but don't want to admit it, that they fear that we might also have a compelling literary argument, that the stories we tell and the way we tell them are right and that they're getting it wrong.

And though I have spent all these years as a writer, have had all the training in the craft, got all these ideas in my head, I have watched my friend Lenore and felt compelled to overcome my own hesitations to support her, with admiration, awe, and perhaps a touch of envy. The me who writes a lot about spirits, well, ghosts anyway, has never had anything close to a paranormal experience, not that I feel I need or want one, but the way Lenore's grown since her time with that medicine woman, what power she has now, what an artist she is when she tells. Talk about working spells with words. Talk about reaching our community. Christianized, university-trained, the reality-based me — "colonized," maybe? — also wants to tell stories, feels uneasy with the role the writer plays, the writer who steals, the writer who tries to lie truthfully (this last conundrum in apparent defence of the writing practice in the face of imperial empiricism).

This unease began surfacing a few years back after Gwendolyn MacEwen — remember her? — died. I'd bought her last book, had luxuriated in its sure music, the way it addressed the darkness as, I thought, an equal. She seemed to me then — one sees what one wants to see — the embodiment of what I thought a writer ought to be, an artist who can take the measure of our several lives. I thought, I hoped, that this was but the first step of her maturity. And then she was gone and rumours went around that she had done herself in with drinking. Friends who had been friends of hers — I had never met her — had been out of town. And she had been so alone and poor. You can't eat off a poetry best seller. You can't trade a Governor General's Award in as collateral.

This exotic, beautiful, talented, probably wounded woman was suddenly one of those writers who had always been my oppressors. The dead writers denied the existence of Indians. Their worlds were complete without us. I looked at her last book again, saw her address the darkness not as an equal but as her controlling lover, that romantic dead end. And then I read again her poem "The Names" and took it personally. It goes:

> *We want to pretend that you are our ancestors—*
> *you who are called*
> Wolf in the Water, Blue Flash of Lightning, Heaven Fire,
> Black Sleep—
>
> *You who have no devil, no opposite to Manitou.*
>
> *You who are hiding behind your names, behind*
> *closed doors of thunder*
> *And will not let us in.*

Backlit by blue lightning, the silhouette of the wolf
    drinks the midnight river; fire from heaven
Falls on our sleep and invents morning; the air is thick
    with feathers from surreal birds.

You who never knew the evil in us, you who have
    no opposite to Manitou,
Come out from behind the thunder and embrace us—
All we long to become, all we have never known of
    ourselves.

Before you are gone from our eyes forever—
    (you who are certainly not our ancestors)
Teach us our names, the names of our cities.

No one ever welcomed us when we came to this land.

And then I thought, "Oh, give me a break, Gwendolyn. One
ought not to speak ill of the dead, but what a load of crap. We not
only welcomed you, we fed you, we clothed you, we told you
names like *Canada, Toronto, Saskatchewan, Quebec.* We told you
what they meant. We never hid, and we saw and see the evil in
you too clearly. Talk about Wounded Knee, talk about Oka, why
don't we! You just refused to listen, to assume this land and its
names and what they mean as your own. Even after all these
generations, you still take your vacations in Europe or wherever
it is you think the Old Country is, as if you believe still that there
is no history, nothing to see here. Now we can talk about real
perversity."

And suddenly I saw her and her ilk as seductive but seduced
by the popular image of the writers as a sort of solitary, spiritual
explorer, a pioneer for the empire, expendable but therefore entirely heroic, romantic. I saw her then again alone in her room,

posed before 'the wilderness of the page, the yawning abyss' so many writers talk about, gathering her courage to descend again into the Other, which is only a part of her self.

Thanks a lot, Gwen.

No wonder she drank. We social animals use solitary confinement as a punishment. Yet all we tell our best writers suggests that they can gain their special powers by putting themselves in solitary. No wonder most writers claim to hate writing, would rather socialize. But is the writer's working solitude any more difficult than, say, the working solitude of the cabinetmaker? Why do we say it is? The job is to make sense of chaos. The working of it comes from the energy of anguish. The finished order is beautifully its own reward.

Also in that last book one can look at MacEwen doing a bit of clowning around, answering what she calls 'The Question':

> *The question is Why Do You Write.*
>
> *Every time I hear The Question I get this*
> *purple blur in front of my eyes, and*
> *I fear I will fall down frothing at the mouth*
> *and spewing forth saliva and*
> *mixed metaphors.*
>
> *You can study it if you want, I'm*
> *just the one who gets to do it; or,*
>
> *Don't ask me I just work here.*
>
> *You know the answer and still I have to say it:*
>
> *Poetry has nothing to do with poetry.*
> Poetry *is how the air goes green before thunder,*

is the sound you make when you come, and
why you live and how you bleed, and

The sound you make or don't make when you die.

It is a beautiful, Romantic answer — life and death, madness, passion, an edge of irony, an urge toward oblivion, complex and artful.

My own response to The Question must be simpler. I've watched my friend and many other storytellers. I've seen the faces of their listeners. In the process, I've measured my own relationship to words. And always there is one thing present — pleasure. One has to enjoy words to tell stories, to make them heard, to remember and have them remembered. And that is what storytelling is about — memory and remembering. Memory work for grown-ups is play and the work I want to do.

Writing, on the other hand, is hard work, is painful. Everybody says so.

Since I'm no longer quite so Christian, quite so young, am specifically a Delaware from the Six Nations reserve — no longer satisfied with that vague and misplaced designation "Indian" — I have decided that writing then must be about forgetting, oblivion, and given — no, taking the choice between that and pleasure, I have decided it would be better to forget all about it.

My answer to The Question now is that I don't write. I tell stories.

(1991)

SILENCE (?) (!) (.)

My first thoughts on receiving the request that I take part in a panel on Silence had to do with that part of language that languishes, unstudied but mysterious, between the period we place at the end of one sentence and the capital letter we use to start the next.

You know, that space on the page that allows us, in reading, a moment for the lungs and the mind to inspire — to take in the spirit of our subject matter (which means, of course, that the other parts of a sentence — let's call them "words" — connect with expiring, not only in the last sigh sense that most obviously lies in the period, but also in the sense of getting the spirit of our subject matter out of our minds and into the air or onto the page).

I mean silences, blanks, places of nullity or neutrality, were, if you can imagine it, my big discovery as an undergraduate. Talk about belabouring the obvious. Rests in music, clear colour in paintings, stillness in dance, silence in drama and poetry. Form versus content turned in my mind from a dichotomy, a conflict, an argument — all concepts I was unconsciously but nevertheless profoundly uncomfortable with in those school years, concepts that were very much central to what I was supposed to be learning to accept — into a process, a tension, a vividness, a constant shifting from foreground to background and back, a strobing of meaning, a concretion, a concatenation of sense. I mean, I'd found myself a little pearl of wisdom. Take a pause, take a breath, take a silence.

And much later I realized I was searching for an aesthetic that fit in with the way I'd been brought up. I mean, for instance, we are taught in mainstream aesthetics that "conflict" is a necessary characteristic of drama. I had difficulty dealing with this because at home we were taught not to fight. How was I supposed to write a play if I thought that conflict was more a failure of imagination than an adequate expression of emotion? I now use a different qualification for perhaps the same sorts of situations: I write plays full of "contrast."

And what better contrast than that between words and silence?

These, more or less, were my first thoughts on Silence.

Then I got the letter to confirm the panel and a requested paper — not a poem. Was that supposed to be an example of genre silencing? I wasn't sure I understood the intent of the accompanying suggested topics: gender identity, colour, genre, myth.

Am I blue? Aren't these tears in my eyes telling you?

I mean, I don't normally spend time as an essayist. Whose jargon is this anyway? Then I realized what was wanted was Native politics or history, that I was supposed to be a representative of Canada's First Nations, that I was — not again! — the liberal's token Indian.

Hey, who elected me Chief?

As I said above, we're taught not to fight, we do not value conflict, and though I dislike feeding into any discussion of race (from my perspective our differences are in our cultures, thank you very much), I decided I would try to think again:

Indian culture? What do you want to know about that for? It won't do you any good.

My grandmother, my father's mother, who died last October at the age of ninety-five, said that to me, way back years ago when she was much alive, when she was a lady and I myself was little more than a child.

A woman who spent her last years lying in bed, drifting toward death, losing flesh as if it were her memory, growing small — but not like a child.

On a typical visit, I'd say: *Do you know who I am?*

And after a moment, she'd say, *Oh yes.*

Who?

Silence.

Had she forgotten?

Or could she have been withholding her words, like a child whose only power lies in refusal?

It won't do you any good.

And I thought, "No, I don't want to talk about Indian this or that."

I thought that my grandmother was right about Indian culture, at least if it's the history and politics of race and property and pain. Owning that will gain me nothing.

So if you want it, here, I give it to you. Not that it's really mine to give. That story's yours, certainly. You who can choose to put me in this position. Maybe Indian culture will someday belong to all of us, be ours.

But some owning up to it needs to be done first.

And there were other thoughts having to do with silence and the experience of it, ideas both social and aesthetic, ideas autobiographical and personally political. But they belong to some Delaware from the Six Nations lands who realizes now that this is not the place for them and that he's come as far along the backtrack as he can.

Do you know who I am? he asks. *Who?*

(1992)

THE OTHER'S SITUATION?

An Apology

I'm sorry to say, after too many days spent worrying the idea over and over, that there does not appear to be any way I can get my "self" much interested in the project of "siting the other."

Even my perspective here, at what appears just off-centre in the landscape of Canadian drama (I'm writing in Toronto), does not yield any vistas that invite. The "other" is just so far away, across a grand river, and then too many hours' drive . . .

I remember that I used to be more curious about what lay out there, what that glow bigger than a full moon about to rise over the horizon at dusk was all about. But I was younger then and, believing what I had been taught, that curiosity about the "other," the unknown, was just part of our universal human nature and that that place across the line had to be explored, discovered, if I wanted to grow up and be a man.

And what did going along with that, going off into that territory, get me?

Other than certification in some too small circles, a couple of university degrees, only some time as a thrilled country boy in the rich strangeness of the cities that gave off the glow, some bits of beginning knowledge of that so-called universal common culture, a sense of the placement on the map of international masterpieces and classics that define the sanctified valleys and heights, the plains and lakes of the western or, at least, English-speaking world's theatre.

(Shakespeare and Chekhov and Beckett to mention, as a gesture of reassurance to the reader, just the holy locations I haven't yet and probably won't ever be able or capable of losing track of as long as I'm still resident on that westernized world side of the line, at least within part of my educated, righted mind.)

All of which impressed and excited and oppressed me. How beautiful and awesome and strange.

But when I had learned enough, saw how I too might change to stone, to landscape, to well-known territory, I stopped, feeling I was about to be lost, despite the assurances of the map. It was all just too far from home.

And so I backtracked, stepped with at least my left foot back across the line onto reserve land. Curiosity did not quite kill this cat, but it sure slowed him down.

Now whatever exists of my curiosity finds its focus within the confines of a homebody. My home territory is more than curious enough to keep me interested and centred.

Now at my middle-of-life age the particulars of a world of friends, not strangers, who are in varying combinations members of groups located in the directions of family, aboriginals, artists, and two-spiriteds, is more than territory enough for me, although exploring and discovering it seems unnecessary when what strategies I hope to realize have to do with defence, with allowing it and my "self" to survive in some sort of state of balance.

I mean just how can the "other" compete with that? From here, across those uninviting vistas, it all appears to be beyond not only my interest but my understanding:

A theatre critic calls across the river with what he considers a friendly question: When are you going to write a mainstream play?

A well-meaning bourgeois suggests: It would be amazing to see Graham Greene and Gary Farmer as *The Odd Couple*!

Another wonders: When will we be seeing Graham Greene at Stratford as Lear?

And it's so pleasing that Native Earth Performing Arts and Cahoots Theatre Projects and Buddies in Bad Times Theatre, for instances, exist so that there are places for the Indians and immigrants and queers to play, respectively, because, well, they're not really Canadian theatre now, are they?

And Shakespeare is our summer theatre.

And a Disney-scrubbed musical brought up from down on the Great White Way gets the officials and audiences out . . .

Perhaps all of Canadian theatre is marginal?

Meanwhile, the task of expressing my "self" as a twenty-first century First Nations person, reclaiming and reviving, for myself and my circle, what is still viable in our traditions and inventing whatever else is needed, is so much more interesting — who has the time to attend to whatever it is the "others" are on about?

(1993)

WORDS AND ENTROPY

A Trickster-ish Memoir

1.

It gets hot in Oklahoma.

The week I was there in the summer of 1992, the temperature in Fahrenheit never went below 80, even at night.

And the days were clear and endlessly burning, the sun, in memory now, always turning in place overhead, the better to pull the red or the mercury up through the degrees of the thermometers.

Where I come from in southern Ontario, we're used to two or three weeks in the 80's every summer, and there's at least two or three days in those weeks when, for a few hours, the wave of heat crests the 90's and, even for those of us raised there, it becomes too hot to think, too hot to work.

Imagine then how it felt to be visiting Norman, Oklahoma, where every day the temperature approached a hundred.

Every day I had to hurry across the well-watered greens of that prairie university campus, had to hurry between the air-conditioned buildings, trying to avoid getting that temperature too, to avoid settling into a sweaty, dead-headed stupor.

I was there, whatever the weather, on business, a writer at a writers' conference.

I needed to keep what wits I had about me.

But since I was there as a Native writer at that conference called "Returning the Gift" and since all the other writers, over six hundred professional and student, were also Native, it felt more like a celebration, whatever the weather.

It was hard not to be excited, feverish, at least in an intellectual way.

There was so much to hear, so much to say, too many unfamiliar familiar faces, so much that didn't need to be said.

It had never been like that for me before, at a writers' conference.

I wasn't there to explain myself.

We were there to explain each other.

It felt like coming home, despite the heat, the sun, despite the rusty colour of the soil we continually remarked on.

Only on the last day did clouds come along, did the heat moderate, that last day when we rode out across red-earthed Oklahoma three hours by bus, out of the prairies and into a landscape of hills, lakes, green trees, to be guests at the Sac and Fox Powwow.

It gets hot in Oklahoma, so hot, at powwows, they don't dance by day. They do everything else you might want to do at powwows — they eat, they shop, they flirt and tease, they laugh and gossip — but dancing they don't do till after dusk.

By the time of the Grand Entry, the sky was clearing, all purple and gold, and I was sitting, crowded to the top of the bleachers, at the edge of a field big enough to play a game of football on.

I think there must have been eighteen or twenty drums around it, and two or three of them, like me, were visiting from Canada.

I also almost seem to remember torches, although I'm sure there was a flood of electric light.

"Welcome to the heart of Indian country!" the caller's voice came over the PA system.

And veterans of wars were leading the way, carrying the Stars and Stripes, the Maple Leaf, the standards of the local tribes.

Oklahoma's full of Indians from all over the eastern half of America.

I live in Ontario but have distant Delaware relations there.

The American Diaspora that night was in evidence in all the names announced, all the tribes, the nations.

Imagine all those men, women, the children, each one of them dancing into that field in his or her turn, imagine all those outfits, the fabrics, the leather, all the colours, all the beads and bells and feathers, imagine all the different songs, the rhythms, the drums, imagine all this coming together until that entire field was full to overflowing, was turning, a spiralling community dancing under the stars in their constellations, that hot Oklahoma night.

2.

There are two things I know I learned, or was reminded of, at that conference.

The first, I immediately knew would help me in my work as a writer.

I'd been on a panel titled "Entering the Canons: Our Place in World Literature," along with four other people, including Kimberly Blaeser, an Anishnabe woman who teaches at the University of Wisconsin in Milwaukee.

She delivered a paper that included the following ideas:

> ... Native Americans have a distinct ... voice ... that speaks about ... "homing in", ... about natural cycles, spiritual connections, family, community and place ... an interesting theory of Valentin Volosinov ... seems ... to help illuminate the place and significance of Native American literature, and ... draws connections between the work of native peoples throughout the world. ... He identifies two basic styles of writing: the linear or monologic associated with the ruling classes, and the dialogic or pictorial associated with the

under or working classes. The first, the linear, he says, "draws hard, clearly demarcated boundaries" and "tends to move toward purity and unity." The second, the dialogic, is "a mixture of popular and unofficial genres, full of the voices of other people," it "infiltrates boundaries and blurs established genres," and "tends to mix texts and their authority." The second, of course, quite accurately described the characteristic style of Native American writing ....

That seemed to me to be a description of my own work — if not of its accomplishment at the time, then certainly of its tendency.

I mean once I'd finished it, I hadn't been satisfied with the singular lyrical voice of *Delicate Bodies*, my first book of poems.

That individual expression had seemed to me too limited.

I'd wanted to write something with a bit more of society in it.

So I found myself moving more and more often in the poems into an ironic stance that implied other voices and dialogues.

And, of course, I'd found myself finally writing plays.

So, after the panel I went right up to Kimberly and asked her for a copy of the paper, thinking it would at least help me explain something about my work to my director and actors.

The second thing I eventually discovered I was carrying around after that conference was that memory of the Grand Entry under the night sky.

Eventually, I vaguely realized that memory and the ideas from Kimberly's paper were practically the same thing.

3.

I was preparing then to write a new play, the third in what's become a cycle of plays exploring the place of Native people in this modern world of cities.

After that week in Oklahoma I suddenly needed to, some-how, put the energy I'd felt in that Grand Entry into the play.

So I came up with a sprawling script my director was sure would run for four hours.

But "Kyotopolis" — that's a Coyote-spirited Metropolis — was thick because of descriptions of images and special effects, not dialogue, and when we eventually workshopped it with a student cast it ran a bearable two hours.

It's a dark fantasy that begins when the space shuttle carries a Native woman into orbit and into the obituaries.

It also includes scenes in a Belgian castle, a Hawaiian volcano, and a flying saucer.

It's a mystery that's never solved because the detective can't or won't listen to all the stories and all the different ways the storytellers in the play tell them.

I mean, I found myself playing around with storytelling, reminiscing, reporting, monologues, dialogues, diatribes, dreams — and we used live action, live video, prerecorded video, pirated video, slide projectors, video projectors, lasers . . .

The play's a medley of ways of communicating.

I think of it most succinctly as a sort of literary shamanic journey about the Native Global Village.

I wasn't sure the thing held together, even though it seemed the epitome of Kimberly's "mixture of popular and unofficial genres, full of voices of other people."

I'd doubted it, even though I'd built into the thing a solid narrative structure just like the one in *Citizen Kane*.

I doubted it because I'd never tried anything like it before.

It was only when I saw it in that student production that I began to understand what I'd done, began to have some confidence in it, even though a lot of the critics in the audience felt the play didn't make sense, that it was kind of, well, chaotic.

But what's wrong with chaos anyway?

I mean, just what is the problem?

Once I started to think about it, I realized that this question of the chaotic was intriguing.

I realize that usually the chaotic gets identified with all that's bad in the world and beyond it, us versus the Devil, that anarchy's a four-letter word and that everything can and must be understood and controlled, or what's modernity for?

Well, I suggest to you that this question of the chaotic may well be one of the primary questions to consider in understanding the difference between the Native and the modern world views.

I can, at least, attest that this difference is the one that is currently of some fascination to me.

It's a fascination that has grown out of a frustration, a frustration that is partly my own fault.

Partly it's also, I suspect, a quality of this moment in history we've all living in and making.

About this time of year, eight years ago, I got a good idea.

I'd been working and writing in the city of Toronto for a half-dozen years then.

I had met and worked with a circle of other Native writers that formed around the writer/story teller Lenore Keeshig-Tobias.

And I'd begun working with the bunch of artists and community members who showed up in answer to a cry for help from Tomson Highway.

And we not only helped him save the Native actors' theatre, Native Earth Performing Arts, but also began transforming it into a theatre for Native writers.

And I saw that the work we were doing was really good and thought it deserved more attention.

I'd also noticed another literary group in the city getting attention just because they were a group.

So I thought we too should organize and I invited my colleagues Lenore and Tomson to a meeting.

But what, after all, could a Cree musician and playwright (Tomson), an Ojibwa storyteller (Lenore), and a Delaware poet with Iroquoian roots (me) agree to agree on?

It wasn't as bad as the constitutional negotiations.

We are artists, after all.

What we came up with was a rather rich irony.

We came up with the Committee to Re-Establish the Trickster.

You see, it seemed to us that this "Indian" label we've all been saddled with was, at best, a stereotype.

How seriously can you get taken as a human being if people think you're heroic or stoic or romantic or a problem?

So seriously you lose your humanity.

We wanted people besides ourselves to be dissatisfied with the stereotypes.

We didn't think they were doing anybody any good.

They certainly weren't doing us as Native writers any good.

You get tired of being told your work doesn't measure up because it doesn't quite conform to the stereotypes.

For a ridiculous but all too typical instance, I once had someone tell me my short story "King of the Raft" wasn't credible because everyone knows that Indians don't play games, let alone chess.

Indians do play chess.

Or, at least, this Indian did as a kid.

And certainly games of skill and prowess, like lacrosse, and games of chance — hey, where do you think the stereotype of the Bingo-loving Indian got its start? — were an integral part of traditional societies.

I once did some very preliminary research on the subject of games in traditional societies and came up with all sorts of suggestive information about gambling.

There were games that used dice in bowls, that used music and counters, and teams and sleight of hand.

I imagined a feast in any Native village would have had much the same energy as the Rama Casino.

Truth is stranger than ignorance, stranger even than fiction.

Now, doesn't that seem like a problem with, or for, fiction?

Which one of the Greeks stuck us with our current definition?

It's not like you can change the truth, take the strangeness out of it, at least in a democracy.

And why would you want to manage truth that way, anyway?

Variety seems to be more than the spice of life.

It seems, in a democracy, it would be the main course.

So why not shift your fiction more strangely toward the truth?

That's all we wanted to accomplish.

To open up a space for a little bit of the strange but true about us.

That we've been labelled "Indians" is your problem.

We chose, to lever open that space, a tool some anthropologist or ethnologist had come up with — digging around through our stories, taking them apart, sorting those parts and slapping labels on everything, one of those labels being the category archetype, with a subheading "Trickster."

We hoped that if this Trickster character was strange enough to a scientist to be marked and remarked upon, then it might also be true enough to get us all beyond the scientific attention span.

It also didn't hurt that the Trickster as we knew him, as Coyote or Weesageechak or Nanabush, as Raven or Glooscap, was as shifty and shiftless, as horny and greedy, as lucky, as funny, as human as any of us.

So we took that archetype and started waving it around, the banner of our Committee to Re-Establish the Trickster.

And for the next while, a couple years, we did lectures and workshops, even put out a couple issues of a little magazine dedicated to the idea that the Trickster was emblematic of a different world view and the different literature connected to it.

And suddenly it seemed to us that, through our efforts and the efforts of a lot of other Native artists, the Trickster had become very *au courant*, re-established.

People wanted to be in the know about the little fellow.

Yes, we'd accomplished what we'd set out to do.

I mean, graduate students had started playing Spot the Trickster — which was good, wasn't it?

It was — except that it seemed they assumed that once they had located him, they'd know all there was to know about Native literature.

But look at him, folks.

If spotting the Trickster prepares you for Native Literature, then spotting the Fool is all you need to know about Shakespeare.

My friend Lenore contends that the Trickster teaches us what *not* to do.

His appreciation, then, always demands that adult, ironical stance.

Somehow, he's always other than what you expect — neither hero nor villain, not quite your anti-hero either, always shifting through and beyond our categories.

Definitely a force to be reckoned with.

And giving Jack a name won't necessarily keep him in the box.

Maybe we should have been wiser in the first place, considered the source, known that the Trickster might be too simple a sign, might just be another case of 'Indian' all over again.

My frustration was the realization that hardly anybody was getting much beyond the surface.

I think I can understand that.

That surface can be pretty shifty after all, can seem to be dangerous.

There always seemed to be an edge of irritation or discomfort or even fear in the voices of those graduate students, as if they didn't quite know how to handle something that couldn't be, wouldn't be, clearly defined.

I recognized, or rather remembered, that range of feelings from my own experience.

That was the way I felt the first time I came across and tried to understand, back when I still had required science courses, the idea of entropy.

Yes, here we are at the word "entropy."

Entropy's an old idea, coined by a German physicist sometime in 1800s.

It's supposed to be a measure of the *dis*order in a system.

Isn't it terrible that that seems a terribly Germanic concept?

It also seems a terribly modern one.

Entropy, disorder, is supposedly always on the increase.

Cosmologists suggest that eventually the entire universe will run down, energy-less, changeless, that we'll all turn into a lukewarm gas, if you'll pardon the image.

They use the phrase "heat death."

Which makes me think again about Oklahoma, but without air conditioning.

But in the meantime, we do have air conditioning.

In this world we have all sorts of things and engage in all sorts of activities, like writing, that seem to resist disorder.

We're always putting things in rows, measuring them, categorizing them.

We even do it to each other.

Even our physical senses are primed to see patterns and then we provide meanings for them.

Think again of the constellations.

Maybe it's in our human nature to be anti-entropic creatures.

I mean, why else would we have taken up the idea of entropy, of measuring disorder, of making sense *even* out of chaos?

But how would one do that anyway?

Well, practically speaking, you could talk about the amount of energy *un*available for work in a system.

In a car, for instance, measure the heat the engine gives off, the stuff that's generated by friction and inefficiency, that doesn't drive the vehicle, the stuff that's going to waste.

In information and communication theory, look for a measure of the uncertainty of the information contained in a message and then look for ways to minimize it.

You don't want to have to worry, after all, about static changing the balance in your bank account.

Let's also apply that idea of entropy as a measurement of uncertainty to our purposes as writers.

Would that mean, for instance, that prose would have less entropy than poetry?

That would certainly explain why poetry seems so much harder, sometimes, to write, to get right — because it needs to have a certain measure of the wrong in it.

And if we look for entropy in other parts of our work, in plot, say, or dialogue or narrative, in description or character, it seems to me we'll discover that what looks like a measure of disorder from the outside feels very much from the inside like what we casually call "creativity."

Let me recall a moment from a conversation with a friend who wanted to know what it felt like to write creatively.

She was sure she couldn't do it, being an academic, but she did coax the following image out of me.

I told her writing felt to me like jumping off a cliff with a sealed box, praying that it contained the parts, at least, of a parachute, hoping it might hold the wings of a glider, knowing that I had to put whatever it was together if I didn't want to hit bottom.

So, you enter chaos and try to find a new order in it, she suggested.

I thought that was a great analysis.

That sounds kind of scary, she said, and I had to admit, though it seemed almost silly to say it, that it was.

Chaos, entropy.

Scary as a Trickster, I'd have to say, because these were just two of the ideas almost nobody seemed to be talking about or interested in, ideas that little fellow the Trickster, whatever you call him, seems to me to be an embodiment of.

4.

Fluttering among the whirling images that begin and end my play *Kyotopolis* is the image of a yellow butterfly.

At first, I thought the image was only pretty or sentimental — it's connected to a scene evoking an idyllic childhood.

I thought I might even try to edit that butterfly out, just being practical, not wanting to drive my designer crazy.

But once I heard the reactions to the play, the description of it as *chaotic*, I realized the butterfly was there as a fair warning to the audience of the atmosphere the play operates in and partakes of.

We, after all, live in a world that's recently welcomed into the popular imagination the ideas of chaos theory, most particularly the idea of the butterfly effect.

Chaos theory suggests that some phenomena are just too complex to ever accurately predict — the weather, for instance.

But the theory also suggests that patterns, nevertheless, can be detected.

The seasons, the climate, for instance, are patterns one can see in weather.

However, the butterfly effect suggests that, in systems this unpredictable, even the smallest causes can have great effects.

So that a butterfly fluttering by today may stir up a tornado by next Thursday.

What may be most appealing about this chaos stuff is that it suggests that there are limits to the way science has taught us to understand and bureaucracies have told us to control the world.

Some economists, for instance, want to apply these ideas to the economy.

To me, what's appealing in chaos theory is that it seems to be the new home of the mysterious, the spiritual.

To me, matter is not all that matters.

I also like the theory because it shows me I'm not the only one who's seeing chaos everywhere.

I think we're all of us looking for a way out of modernity, have been ever since it gave us the Holocaust.

And we are approaching the end of the millennium.

This expectation is part of the mythology.

Something's got to give.

I wonder if you could take, for example, the characteristics our more academic colleagues ascribe to the postmodern and have them make sense in a literary version of chaos theory.

You'd probably talk about things like mixing up popular and unofficial genres with the voices of other people, about crossing boundaries and blurring established distinctions.

It all seems so familiar I'm reminded that one of the workshops I never got asked to do for the Committee to Re-Establish the Trickster was to have been titled "Post-Modern and Prehistoric: Can they co-exist?" Who cares?

But I do know now that I'm not alone in art in my fascination with chaos.

A prime example of a writer who's exploring this region where Native traditions of storytelling and chaos seem to overlap is the mixed-blood Anishnabe writer Gerald Vizenor.

Even on the level of content, in novels like *Bearheart: The Heirship Chronicles* and *The Heirs of Columbus,* Vizenor shows a traditional story about a game of chance at the supernatural centre of a life-and-death situation.

Another example I chanced upon and helped workshop this past summer is *Sticks and Bones*, a play in progress by Micmac artist Teresa Marshall.

In the play a character named Majig recalls her grandmother's description of the traditional gambling game called waltes:

> "The waltes bowl is the doorway to the centre of the earth,"
> she'd say. "That's where we were all born out of." ... The
> bowl was made out of stone. I remember seeing the old
> people playing. It had a hole in the middle so that the wind
> could pass through. The Wind was Glooscap's helper. ...
> Mostly spirits used to play. They'd take ordinary trees and
> transform them into playing sticks. They said the sticks
> were magic. They had faces carved into them so that the
> spirits from the four directions could play too. ... The spir-
> its would watch to keep the players honest. Honest Indians,
> that's where the term came from. ... I remember she used
> to say that the spirits would help the people lift the bowl
> up and bang it down so that the dice would spin. ... The
> dice represented all the elements of this world: wealth,
> wind, fire, air, two-legged, the winged spirits, trees and so
> on. Depending on how they would land, face up or face
> down, that's how many bundles of sticks you won.

I also chanced upon the following, non-Native example in my summer reading.

In *Angels in America,* Tony Kushner's visionary play, in a scene in heaven, a rabbi is asked why everyone there plays cards:

> In Heaven, everything is known. To the Great Questions are lying about here like yesterday's newspaper all the answers. So from what comes the pleasures of paradise? *Indeterminacy!* Because mister, with the Angels, those makhers, may their names always be worshipped and adored, it's all doom and gloom and give up already. But still is there Accident, in this pack of playing cards, still is there the Unknown, the Future. You understand me? It ain't all so much mechanical as they think.

And speaking of mechanical, we, of course, all know that even our governments are getting familiar with chaos, using gambling for raising money despite traditional objections to the practice which mostly seem to focus around how it all undermines God and the work ethic.

Whatever are we coming to?

So many possibilities, so many openings.

But let me close with something Douglas Cardinal wrote in *The Native Creative Process,* his book with Jeannette Armstrong:

> Love is what makes things move. Love is what makes things powerful. You can't order the universe but you can find what the natural forces are in it that you need in order to do things right. You must allow yourself to be comfortable with chaos and dependent on it to get things done. To deliver a dream to reality you must allow yourself to be vision-oriented, using all means positive to be total. You then have the opportunity to bring powerful things to bear in a non-adversarial way, asking for the contributions of all others and things.

Which all sounds to me like the how and why of a powwow, say, coming together, a community dancing, spiralling under the sun, or even under the stars in their constellations, on a hot Oklahoma night.

(1994)

HOW MY GHOSTS GOT
PALE FACES

My first play, *Coyote City*, began in darkness. Then the voice of a man said:

Give me a drink. I need a drink. Shit, I'm over here, you bugger.

Then a light came up, letting the audience see that he was a young man, an Indian man.

He continued his monologue, talking to someone who, it seemed, stood just beyond the light:

I'm almost empty here. Come on and dispense with the booze.

Please man, I'm good for it. You can trust me. I'll pay you tomorrow first thing. Come on. Come on, man, really.

Hey you want my knife? It's a real beaut. Look at all the things, man, the gadgets. Hey you can even cut your toenails. Come on, guy, just one more beer. Shit.

Hey, how about a date with a real doll? Shit man, she's fresh from the bush. I'll give you her number. Real pretty Indian chick. What do you say? What do you say?

How about a story my Grandad gave me? A real good story, man. A love story. Come on, man, the ladies really love to hear this story. Shit, it gets them all loose. You like loose ladies, don't you? Just another beer, man, just one. That's all.

The. first time I got invited back to my alma mater, the Vanier College of York University in Downsview in the northwest corner of metropolitan Toronto, to read from my work, I read from this piece, and one of the students, a fair-skinned, dark-haired young man, asked me whether or not I thought I was exploiting stereotypes of Native people. He sounded angry.

I was surprised by his reaction.

It was as if he hadn't heard my introduction to the piece, as if he hadn't heard the whole piece itself, only heard, say, the first part of the section I've so far shared here with you.

My introduction explains that my inspiration for the play came partly from a story my friend the poet, storyteller and children's author, Lenore Keeshig-Tobias had come across one day in her reading and shared with me. It's a story from the Nez Perce called "Coyote and the Shadow People," a story in which Coyote's love for his deceased wife is almost strong enough to bring her back to life, almost good enough to guide the pair of them across the barren lands between that land of shadows, the land of the dead, to this world of light where people like us all live.

And since it is a Coyote story, my introduction emphasized the "almost."

I would also have probably told those students how I had known I needed to do something with the story, write something, how I had to find my own way to tell it, that something in me knew how important that journey to the land of the living was even when I was first reading it. I knew it was beautiful.

My introduction would have also admitted that it took me a long time to find my way to do that, partly because my everyday world of part-time jobs and subway rides took up a lot of time — I was still working security at the Art Gallery of Ontario — but mostly because I felt the distance between that archetypical story of love and death and my everyday world seemed too far a journey for me to make. How do you connect an eternal truth with dry-cleaning receipts? How do you bring the land to the city?

My introduction might also have mentioned that it was one of my favourite people, my sister, who happened to push me my first few steps along the path of that journey.

She lives in another city, and was associating then with people who I felt had an unhealthy interest in what the tabloids call the "paranormal." One day in October she telephoned and, after reminding me with her characteristic bluntness that her birthday was approaching, inquired whether I might like a suggestion as to what her present from me might be.

What she wanted was a book, which pleased me, because she's not been much of a reader since she got out of school, much to my professional chagrin. However, the one she requested was whichever book Shirley Maclaine had at that time lately released. And she wanted the hardcover, didn't want to wait for the paperback. So I found myself down at the local occult bookstore, buying it for her, feeling vaguely embarrassed but also reasonably sure that no one I knew would see me there. And as I stood in line, the Maclaine volume in hand, waiting to pay, there on a shelf of books beside the cash register I noticed the title *Phone Calls from the Dead*.

Yes, there was an entire paperback book composed of stories gathered from hundreds of people who had felt the reach and touch of someone from beyond.

And the image of a phone call from a ghost became my direction into that play. How clearly it made the connections I needed for that long-distance call from the city to eternity, for that return ride the characters of the play take from the land to the now. And it seemed to me then suddenly so obvious and true, this extraordinary experience all these regular people knew.

Of course, in my own head, I admit, I kept using the word "folklore," as if what the folks, what people know, shouldn't be counted for too much.

Telling that story there in the bosom of my university, I may even have taken the opportunity to point out that my having spent six years getting a higher education, even if it was more or less in the direction of the fine art of writing, had not really prepared me for dealing with what would only be described by my university-trained rationality as irrational.

I doubt that my introduction would have admitted that my dilemma at the time was that this lovely story that had me in its grip was in essence a ghost story and I knew that we all know that ghosts, well, they just don't really exist now, do they? At least not like they did back then, when we didn't know science. Don't we share a different reality now?

Somehow I wasn't entirely ready to accept what any educated person would see was only anecdotal evidence.

No, I wasn't at all ready to accept the story.

I did admit to myself that maybe my heart was sort of possessed by "the spirit of the story," but in my head, over too much of the time it took to develop the play, I admit, I kept using the word "metaphor" as if a literary label could control the thing.

It didn't much help me deal with this edge of reality I found myself compelled to explore that the first director I worked with on the piece, as I remember it, would direct the actors' attention to each scene in which the ghost appeared by singing the theme to *The Twilight Zone*.

I wish now I'd been confident enough to mutter to her something like: "I bet you never get to direct *Hamlet*."

But metaphors don't talk, so I had a hard time writing, until I made one of those imaginative vaults student writers are always encouraged to make, using as a pole the rationale that the ghost in my play was just another character, just a regular guy, a human creature who had to deal with a handicap, being dead but not realizing it.

Thus did I first cautiously touch down in the land of the dead, assuring myself that land was merely literary.

Yes, I had spent all those years schooling my heart to write and my head still thought stories were unimportant!

But in that land I insisted was merely literary, I made or met my first ghost.

But I'm sure my introduction to my reading included none of that worry, included only a slightly ironic apology that I had to give away one of play's little surprises, only because, practically speaking, there wasn't time for me to read all the way into the play to the scene that revealed the truth about Johnny, the young man wanting the drink — that he's that ghost.

And what better explanation could there be for his ability to look through the "fourth wall,"[1] usually so impenetrable to a dramatic character, as he continues his monologue? He'd failed to get a drink from the unseen bartender, so he turned from that light to the darkness where the audience sits and addressed them with the following:

> Acting like I'm not here, like he can't see me. Acting like
> I'm just another drunk Indian. Think he thinks I've had
> enough? Do you think that too? Do you think I've had

---

[1] The fourth wall refers to that barrier that the actors as characters on stage must imagine separates them and their virtual world from the audience.

enough? Enough. Shit. You think I've had too much. Well, who the fuck are you anyway? I don't know you. I don't know you. Shit, you're not even real. I know I need a drink when I meet you. I look at you and I need a drink. Hey, you're nothing but a bunch of spooks. That's why I got the shakes. You're the ones took Coyote in when he went looking for his woman. But no way you're tricking me. No way. I'm too smart for you. You can't get away with all that stuper-shitting with me. You're not going to get away with anything with me. You're going to buy me a drink. Shit ya, you're going to buy me a fucking drink.

The fair-skinned, dark-haired young man had listened but not heard all those words, any of that introduction, did not appreciate the myriad ideas the theatrical context I'd created implied.

I'm sure I replied to his question about stereotypes in the negative, at least in the sense of "exploitation" as unethical.

I probably pointed out that using stereotypical images was one of the conventions, the strengths of the theatre, that when you have only an hour or two to get your story told, you often have to start with the vulgar, easily recognizable version of things, and then do your best to try to shift and enrich it.

Didn't he think that by making the audience face "the drunken Indian" right at the start of the play that I'd get their attention and some of their emotions engaged? Wouldn't the play by then redefining that character as one of the dead suddenly be able to turn their heads around even a little bit? The city of Toronto begins to look a lot like the land of dead! What were these people, my characters, doing there anyway?

I mean, I thought I had created a veritable *coup de théatre*.

But the fair-skinned, dark-haired young man just sat there through the rest of the questions, and I think he must still have been angry, dissatisfied with aesthetic rationalizations, because he left the room immediately afterward, didn't stay to share the free meal the Master of the College and her students had prepared, not what I remember as rational behaviour for the impoverished student.

At one point in the conversation over the lasagna, the Master, in an aside, apologized for the young man. She told me that he'd been in the dark himself until quite recently about his own roots and had been told by his adoptive parents that his biological mother, at least, had been a Native woman, Ojibwa probably. The Master of the College, alma mater herself, told me the young man was very sensitive now about Native issues.

I bet I laughed one of those laughs you get when you start to understand something that puzzles you, when irony is sharp and clear, when the present suddenly connects with history and you feel momentarily sure about what you're doing now and about your future.

It's hard to see around anger.

I wonder if I had known who he was, who he'd so recently become for himself, if I would have been able to tell him what he needed to hear, alive and suddenly alone there in the halls of academe, rawly, uncertainly Indian despite his fair skin?

Saying "It's just a play. Don't let it bother you" or suggesting that the character wasn't necessarily him or me — "You're not looking in a mirror!" — but just a spin on a stereotype, just a metaphor, a probe into a problem, saying those things no longer let me feel smug.

But I still was glad my "drunken Indian" had upset him — and surprised that it had hurt him. Other, older Indians grow tougher skins.

I hope I could have taken him by the hand, given it some version of the shake, and said with sweet, clear irony, something like "Welcome to the race."

I hope my work would finally have encouraged him, raised his spirit.

But in my memory now, he's still fair-skinned, dark-haired, young, but lost like my besotted ghost Johnny in some city, not knowing who his people are or where they come from, not even able to be one with that mixed bunch of people who appear as the audience in the dark theatre, both wanting to get spooked and afraid of it happening.

Since *Coyote City* was produced and published, I have met so many audience members and readers who felt free to tell me their own personal ghost stories, real experiences that can most colloquially be described or explained as seeing ghosts, that I've had to admit that I don't really know what we all know. I now know anecdotal evidence is not unuseful. Yes, I think I'm both envious of those experiences I haven't had and strangely satisfied that there are many things in this life about which I remain in the dark.

Perhaps it's my lack of actual experience that allows me my virtual reality ghosts, my theatrical spooks. I can keep on using them as directions, as probes into my own perceptions, my own quandaries.

"The ghost" is one of those recurring, even haunting images that keep coming into my plays. It seems to be part of what makes my work work. And even when the image of the ghost is not specifically present, there's always something or someone whose very absence is itself part of the play's process.

Maybe the ghost is doing much the same job for me that Coyote does in all the old stories.

While *Coyote City* was running at the Native Canadian Centre of Toronto back in June of 1988, I met another fair-skinned, dark-haired person. She introduced herself as the Artistic Director of a small theatre company that produced work for young people, mostly pieces based on European fairy and folk tales but done up with a lot of ballet and modern dance.

This Artistic Director had already had some success with an adaptation of a west coast tale about Raven stealing the sun and now, enthusiastic about my work, she wondered if, for instance, there might exist an Indian version of a story like *Sleeping Beauty* that I'd be interested in dramatizing for her company.

My first thought was: "Not likely."

I grew up on the Six Nations Reserve, a mostly Iroquoian community on the Grand River lands in southern Ontario. Anthropologists have chosen to describe our traditional culture as matriarchal. Even though the greater part of our population has been Christian for centuries and a lot of our traditional cultural forms have changed, a lot of our values haven't.

So I couldn't imagine even any of the Christian women I knew growing up there doing like a Princess and taking a lie-down to wait for some man to solve her problems. Sometimes I think the women think we men are their problems.

So I told the Artistic Director, "No", and I suspect she was disappointed that the *Sleeping Beauty* story wasn't one of those archetypical, universal stories we've all been taught to look out for as the great ones, but then she, herself, the head of a theatre company, wasn't what anyone would call the helpless female.

Since she'd offered to get me development money from the Ontario Arts Council and since I did need the work then with *Coyote City* a play *accompli*, I added, "But I can make you something."

So I started down along the long path that led to my second play, a one-act called *The Dreaming Beauty* where I would meet another ghost, a woman this time.

I approached the project, at first, rather simple-mindedly, thinking I'd just transplant the story of *Sleeping Beauty* to North America.

My first realization was the dramaturgical one, the fact that a play in which the central character lies down and does nothing but sleep would not be exactly exciting, no matter what continent or culture it came from.

But then I thought about the importance dreams have had for me at points of change in my life, about the value our traditional cultures placed on them and, remembering that there are such things in the dramatic tradition as "dream plays," I knew that my work should be concerned with whatever action was going on in the Beauty's head as she lay sleeping, with the journey she herself was making.

Then I found a version of the *Sleeping Beauty* based on a traditional French text and it was definitely pre-Disney, a long and rather convoluted adventure about a woman's coming of age in a feudal state. Certainly, the prince and love were part of the tale, but so was, for instance, the dilemma of living as a single mother when your husband's gone off fighting a war and nobody in the palace likes you, except for your mother-in-law, and she only likes you because she's an ogress and thinks you and the kids look delicious.

And it seemed that every woman in the story except the Princess had something wrong with her — the fairies were vengeful bitches, the Princess' own mother vain, the ladies-in-waiting gossips — that each was somehow less than properly a woman, and that the story of the *Sleeping Beauty* was a blunt message to little girls that the only kind of woman they should grow up to be was "the Princess."

This, I knew, was not the sort of message I could transplant into Iroquoia unless I was willing to deal with at least being teased for writing the wrong kind of corn.

And part of me also began to worry about more than teasing, about complaints that the media insists come from "radical feminists." "How dare this man," I imagined wan faceless females screeching, "write a story about a woman's identity!"

Well, another part of me had already promised a woman I'd do it and the cheque from the Arts Council was in the bank and, well, most of me was just intrigued by the distance between the fictional feudal world of Princess Aurora and my own living matriarchal democracy. Were there any connections? I began playfully making comparisons, contrasts and decisions.

Of course my first one was that in a democracy, there sure wasn't going to be a Princess. My central character would have to be a sort of Iroquoian *Everywoman*, an Indian any girl.

And maybe I could replace the fairy godmothers, those guides with gifts, with the Three Sisters, characters from our agricultural traditions who embodied the spirits of corn, beans and squash?

And I began to suspect that the evil spell that made everyone fall asleep for a hundred years would in my play have to be something like a nightmare five hundred years, more or less, long, a bad dream — since the Iroquois were an agricultural people — in which winter never left the land.

And then I knew all at once, or decided suddenly, that my play had to be another version of post-Columbian history, an allegory from the Six Nations told as simply as any fairy tale, a dream play about the identity of a young woman who was, perhaps, an embodiment of the Iroquoian people themselves.

But this decision seemed to put the love story out of focus and any Prince, charm notwithstanding, out of the picture.

It seemed to me that in the world of *Sleeping Beauty* the feudal Princess marrying her Prince is a story of upward mobility — she gets to move into his castle and family and become a Queen. The Prince, in the most positive view of the ceremony, becomes, as her husband, magically, her lover, her best friend and protector (in a less sanguine interpretation, he becomes her owner).

But I knew that traditional Iroquois culture was more horizontal and that it was the man who had to change residences to marry, who had to move into his wife's mother's or grandmother's

longhouse. And neither of their political statuses would necessarily change. I also realized that the man, as a new husband,
would, of course, be her lover and, if it so happened, a friend and
the father of her children, but that the young woman's oldest
brother would retain his roles as her best friend, protector and
the protector of her children. (It seems like a practical arrange-
ment for child rearing in view of the fragility of romantic love.)

I realized, then, that using those traditional social structures as
my guides to the play might be troublesome, because it meant that
I needed a character to be a brother, not a lover, and that without
the required romance, a large part of the mainstream audience,
maybe even my Artistic Director, might be disappointed. The play
really would be rooted in one of the differences between the cultures.

But I thought about the Girl as my own sister then and knew
it was right that I write about the Girl's brother too.

My Artistic Director just shrugged away my worries — I don't
think she quite understood. "Oh just be poetic!" she said.

So after most of my women friends assured me that they
trusted me to write about this particular female's identity —
"Look, Dan, you grew up there. You know who our people are."
— the play seemed to just fall onto the page.

Early in *The Dreaming Beauty*, the GIRL searches for clues
to the disappearance of just about everything and everyone she
ever knew underneath the never-ending dream of winter. She
encounters the ghost.

GIRL: ... Hello?

GRANDMOTHER: Child, which way's the cornfield?
I've lost my direction.

GIRL: Granma?

GRANDMOTHER: There's still a couple of hills to be brought in.

GIRL: ... Granma, it's me.

GRANDMOTHER: No use leaving them for the crows. Those birds get more than enough to eat.

GIRL: Granma, look at me.

GRANDMOTHER: Big fat black things, just waiting for me to drop my load.

GIRL: Your hands are so cold.

GRANDMOTHER: Did you know I fell down? They got under my feet.

GIRL: Granma, here's my blanket.

GRANDMOTHER: Child, it won't do no good.

GIRL: Granma?

GRANDMOTHER: That's right, child, you remember.

GIRL: Oh Granma.

GRANDMOTHER: Don't be afraid.

GIRL: I'm not.

GRANDMOTHER: Don't feel sorry for me.

GIRL: I love you, Granma.

GRANDMOTHER: That's good. I love you too. But save your love for them who are alive. They need it more than I do.

GIRL: Oh Granma, what's happening?

GRANDMOTHER: I'm happy here, gathering up the last of the corn. I should have it all in before morning.

GIRL: Where's everybody, Granma? Where'd they go?

GRANDMOTHER: You remember that story, child? Your father coming home at dawn, coming up from the river.

GIRL: When I was born.

GRANDMOTHER: That's why he called you Beautiful Daughter of the Dawn. A good name for a child.

GIRL: That's my name?

GRANDMOTHER: Till you grow up.

GIRL: I didn't know.

GRANDMOTHER: Maybe you forgot. It's easy to forget things as you get older. There's so much to remember. So I made this for you.

GIRL: Oh Granma, it's beautiful.

GRANDMOTHER: The softest deer hide I could make, child. You can keep your medicine inside.

GIRL: I don't have any.

GRANDMOTHER: I know. I was waiting till you grew up to give it to you. But I died first. Stupid birds. But look at this beadwork. The corn design. That's to remind you who I was, how big my house and my fields were.

GIRL: Thank you, Grandmother.

GRANDMOTHER: Promise me you'll grow up sweet and strong like the corn.

GIRL: I'll try, Grandmother.

GRANDMOTHER: Corn silk. Your hair is softer.

GIRL: Granma, wait.

GRANDMOTHER: I have to get back to work.

GIRL: Please stay, Granma.

GRANDMOTHER: It'll all be done by morning.

And the dead Grandmother disappears. My drunk ghost had been one of the lost. Who was this woman?

If the GIRL is an embodiment of the Iroquoian people, then this ghost of a GRANDMOTHER with her cornfields and stories and names and bead- and leatherwork seems to be their culture, still, or maybe simply always, very alive, the Iroquoian spirit there to guide the Beauty back to the land.

It seemed to take the Artistic Director a long time to get together the money to mount *The Dreaming Beauty*. I imagined, or she may even have told me, she was struggling to keep her company financially viable. In the meanwhile I entered the play in a contest.

It also seemed that whenever I would ask her when the production was likely to occur, she would start muttering about the piece not being quite ready really, that she thought I'd not somehow pushed it far enough, that she would give me a call so we could talk about it, a call that never came, I guessed, because she was too busy raising money. Then the play won the contest and the next thing I knew I'd received an invitation to attend the rehearsals, already in progress.

Let's admit that the play had an unfortunate production.

Let's put it down partly to differences in sensibilities and sensitivities rooted in a shared ignorance of each other's cultures.

The young Native actors involved came up to me after the run-through and asked me to talk to her.

Let's just suggest that she didn't quite understand the play.

I remember that the actress playing my good-spirited ghost looked, well, kind of kinky, not grandmotherly at all, in ballet tights and moccasins, and that OLD WOMAN MOON was talking like a banshee. The Artistic Director said she was just trying to make it magical, ethereal. She wouldn't, couldn't accept my suggestion that this spirit of light was more down to earth than that, that the play was about getting back in touch with the land.

I remember my last conversation with that fair-skinned, dark-haired Artistic Director over the telephone included talk about whether or not we were having an argument and that I'd wanted to laugh when I heard her saying: "I have a reputation as an artist, you know!"

Okay, so maybe I had ended up dealing with the Princess after all.

And then one of the actresses injured her ankle and since there wasn't enough money to recast her parts in the play — maybe it all got spent on her big plaster cast — she ended up sitting centre stage to play all her characters, acting like a human Muppet.

I had to let my agent deal with the Artistic Director, warned my friends to stay away, and have managed to be civil when I've encountered her at some other play, even though for me there's something spooky about her now and in her talk of magic and poetry.

Maybe it's simply the absence of a good production of the play that in this instance haunts me.

Or maybe I'm sad, finally having understood just how far folks who live in the city can be from people who live on the land.

The last of my ghosts I want to introduce to you is not just another human character who happens to be dead but is, instead, a rather obviously and intentionally theatrical creature.

I first read a version of the story of Almighty Voice when I was working as a researcher at the Woodland Cultural Centre in Brantford, probably in the fall of 1978. I knew as soon as I came across the story that I would someday do something with it, write something about it. I made a photocopy, started a file.

Almighty Voice was a young Cree warrior who lived in Saskatchewan near the end of the last century. The spiritual sounding name is the English translation of *Kisse-Manitou-Wayou*. His story is usually told by mainstream writers as one of a sad misunderstanding, of a renegade Indian. In the Cree communities of Saskatchewan, the story has a life still that's almost mythical, because Almighty Voice, I know now, became a symbol of resistance.

A short version of the story begins in late October of 1895 when Almighty Voice kills a cow. You don't need to know why, or who it belonged to, if it did, indeed, belong to anyone. All you need to know is that the Mounties hear about it and arrest him and throw him into the guardhouse.

(That guardhouse still stands as a monument to him in the town of Duck Lake. A nearby building sports a mural two stories tall based on the only photograph we believe we have of Almighty Voice.)

Do the Mounties think they will teach him a lesson? Someone among them perhaps thinks he'll just tease Almighty Voice and tells him that he's going to hang for killing the cow. Almighty Voice escapes and heads off across the prairie.

Is the Saskatchewan River already iced over or does he have to ford, even swim, through the freezing waters? One of the Mounties decides to go after the Indian. And there certainly is snow on the ground by the time the Mountie finds Almighty Voice a day or so later, surprises him resting beside a fire.

The details of the incident shift from version to version of the story.

Let's suppose that the Mountie suggests in English that the young man surrender and that Almighty Voice says, "Go away! I won't die for no cow!" in Cree. The result is the death of the Mountie and the start of a manhunt that lasts, off and on, for the next year and a half, with Almighty Voice always managing to elude the authorities, due to his familiarity with the landscape and thanks, no doubt, to his people.

Then in May of 1897, Almighty Voice and two of his friends are spotted by a farmer and chased and cornered in a bluff of poplars. All the authorities, Mounties, soldiers, the priest and the Indian Agent, all of the settlers, farmers, shopkeepers, traders, all the Indians in the area show up to watch the standoff.

Almighty Voice and his friends make like warriors, taunt their
enemies, sing their songs. The authorities try to starve them out
for as long as it takes for the cannons to be brought down from
the fort at Prince Albert. They're small cannons but they work.
Almighty Voice and his friends are killed. The End.

When I first read that story, I guess I was innocent or, more
accurately, ignorant, of the history of that part of Canada. In
school I'd been taught that this country had been settled mostly
by treaty and wasn't that civilized and humane?

How unlike the Americans.

I hadn't realized how much space there might be between the
lines of such documents, hadn't seen the difficulties in translation
between the language of English and, for instance, Cree, between
the respective cultures and sets of values, between, for instance,
what each community thought was the definition of human.

When I first read that story, I was shocked by its arc — kill
a cow and die. I didn't understand what had gone on. I needed
to know more.

I needed to know, for instance, that Almighty Voice was a
young man in the first generation after the Riel Rebellion and
that the site of the Battle of Batoche was in his territory, and that
his was the first generation of people who were confined by
those nice humane treaties on reserves, the first generation of
people for whom the buffalo weren't a major source of food and
inspiration.

Knowing just these instances, one can begin to understand
why a young Cree warrior might kill a cow, how racism started
to be institutionalized, why the whites and their government were
so scared of one dark-skinned delinquent.

Why he might just spark off another uprising out there in
the west!

But when I first started thinking about the story, I hadn't any
of these instances in mind. All I had to think about was that

dark-skinned delinquent and a situation that seemed the epitome of the word "overkill.'

In the different versions of the story I came across over the years, one detail that appeared in a couple of them was the presence at the killing of the Mountie of a witness, a young Cree woman. One version of the story identified her as a cousin of Almighty Voice, travelling with him as a cook. The other version didn't comment on her role at all, only mentioned in a tone of offended astonishment that, after the Mountie was killed, the young woman turned calmly back to tend whatever was cooking on the fire. (How this striking behaviour was observed by no other witness was not revealed.)

Maybe it is because I was raised on the Six Nations, where the power of women has stayed more or less clear, that the presence of the young woman got me thinking. But wouldn't anyone wonder what that young woman thought she was doing there, out in the middle of the winter prairie, away from the village, with that young man and maybe a horse and only the food and weapons they could carry, and at least one Mountie following their trail?

The role of a cook seemed insufficient reason for her to be in such peril, even if she was a relative. Why couldn't he cook for himself? He's a warrior, isn't he? The role of wife or, even more convincing, of lover, however, could make her reasons for being there clear, made the entire situation seem suddenly more interesting.

I remembered then those black-and-white movies that Hollywood put out after the Second World War, movies I'd seen on television late at night that presented the sort of stories where young lovers get in trouble with authority and all the idealism their love implies does them no good at all in the face of stupidity and greed and power.

I realized then that what I was looking at was like those *film noir* stories, love against the odds, *Bonnie and Clyde, Romeo and*

Juliet. That sort of love story was more interesting to me than the renegade Indian one that I'd heard all too often before. I could almost see the logo for "A Universal Picture." So I decided I'd write a story about Almighty Voice and that girl, that my play could be called *Almighty Voice and His Wife.*

I thought it would be fun to find some other version, some other angle, on those shifting but historical facts. I thought it would be both fun and just as important for my own understanding to find some human explanations for what had happened. I thought maybe I'd even manage to sidestep some of those so-called historical facts.

I guess the one historical fact I was most unhappy with was the bloody ending of the story. Most of me knew I was asking for trouble by choosing to write a story which, in fact and by dramatic convention, was tragic — but some small and unreasonable part of me just didn't want to deal with the death of Almighty Voice. Even as I came to understand more of the reasons behind that death, it still seemed too stupid, too grotesque an incident to either acknowledge or imagine. And that part of me also just didn't want to be the one to serve up for public consumption yet another image of the defeated wild Indian.

So I thought I could, and plotted that I would, avoid it.

What I intended to do was to stop the story the moment after Almighty Voice and his friends get cornered in the poplars. I thought I could leave them there and so allow my Almighty Voice at least to go on living forever, a warrior joyously at war. My concept was for a *coup de théâtre* where I'd set the audience up for a tragic death and then surprise them by then forcing their attention away from Almighty Voice and in the direction of all his pursuers.

I wanted to understand what had gone on and thought that a good way to do that would be to get into the heads of those people. (Isn't that what mainstream writers tell us the freedom of the imagination is all about?) So I decided I'd write those characters, those Mounties and soldiers and settlers, and that in that way I'd find out just what they, as individual human beings, thought they were doing to this character I'd started picturing for my own purposes as a sort of Cree James Dean.

It then crossed my mind that if I was going to write all those white characters, then the Native actors I'd worked mostly with till that point would get to play them and that maybe to do that they'd have to wear whiteface. The idea amused me.

I felt lucky that some of the early actor training our company had done was in clown.

I must have known, though, that my plan was too abstract to go through with, too didactic and ideological in a naive sort of way — which is to say, too preachy and smart-assed. I must also have suspected that in the final analysis I couldn't get interested enough in those pale-faced characters as individuals to really create them because, as I set out to do my final historical research in preparation for writing, I found myself also turning over in my mind that image of my Native actors in whiteface.

What I found on its other side was the image of white actors in blackface.

So I also looked into the history and conventions of the minstrel show and discovered that troupes performing these entertainments had travelled across much of North America in the 1800s, not far behind the settlers. A minstrel show was essentially a variety show peopled by caricatures of blacks as happy and stupid on the plantation. The show, of course, was performed by whites.

I wasn't really sure how this connected to the story of Almighty Voice and his wife, but I knew it was important that minstrel shows had still existed at the time Almighty Voice died. It allowed me to suppose that it would not have been impossible that many of the people who gathered to watch the standoff in which

Almighty Voice and his friends were killed had also, in their lives, watched and enjoyed a minstrel show, that their attitudes had been, in part, formed or at least encouraged by the minstrel show's racist stereotypes.

And there was a lot about the crudeness and the strictness of the conventions of the language and the characters used in those shows that fascinated and challenged me. I mean, even though I thought the jokes were hackneyed, part of me still found that the ones that mocked our human capacity for stupidity had the bite of truth.

By this point it was somehow the spring of 1990. I had a pile of research and all these ideas and not one scene on paper. But I was ready and I got lucky, was accepted into the Playwright's Colony at the Centre for the Arts in Banff, Alberta. As I rode the bus from the Calgary airport through the foothills and into the mountains, the first images of the play came into my mind.

A projected title: "ACT ONE: RUNNING WITH THE MOON"

Then another projected title: "SCENE ONE: HER VISION." A drum heartbeats in night's blue darkness. The full moon sweeps down from the sky like a spotlight to show and surround White GIRL asleep in a fetal position on the ground. The drum begins a sneak-up beat, the moon a similar pulse. White GIRL wakes at the quake, gets to her feet, and takes a step. The drum hesitates. A gunshot and a slanting bolt of light stop White GIRL, blocking her path, blocking out the moon. Three more shots and slanting bolts of light come in quick succession, confining her in a spectral tipi. She peers out through its skin of light at Almighty VOICE, a silhouette against the moon. He collapses to the beats of the drum, echoes of the gunshots. White GIRL falls to her knees as the tipi fades and the moon bleeds.

So my first act did tell the entire tragic story as a poetic but straightforward narrative. I couldn't resist the conventions of the tragedy or the love story, both of which seem to require supplies of tears. I did manage at least to find a lyric moment of victory for my warrior in the birth of a son at the end of his year-and-a-half run, just before he goes so bravely to his death.

I'd also found this young woman with the ironic and evocative name of White Girl who, it seemed, had been one of the first from her community to ever be taken away to an industrial — residential — school, to be nearly Christianized. I also knew that she'd had to go on living without him, while the rest of the settling of the west occurred.

And I'd done it all with two actors.

So my second act, titled GHOST DANCE, happened as a vision of my own, probably on the stage of the auditorium of an abandoned industrial school in Duck Lake.

Both the actors were now in whiteface, the man who played Almighty Voice in act one now the GHOST of Almighty Voice, the woman who played White Girl now the INTERLOCUTOR, a white man and the master of ceremonies of something that seemed like the ruins of a minstrel show. The INTERLOCUTOR, though, looked a lot like that Mountie that Almighty Voice had killed in act one and seemed only concerned with getting the GHOST to "toe the line" in the *Red and White Victoria Regina Spirit Revival Show.*

The act re-examined the story of Act One through the non-narrative conventions of the minstrel show, songs, jokes, puns, satire, dance. The clear drama of the act began as the GHOST realized that White Girl still existed inside the character of the INTERLOCUTOR. The GHOST then started to take over the show, to use its conventions to reawaken and remind White Girl about herself.

(Scenes were announced, following the minstrel show convention, through the use of title placards on a tripod.)

The INTERLOCUTOR, fleeing the GHOST, bumps into the placard stand. "SCENE EIGHT: STANDUP" turns up.

GHOST: Sir!

INTERLOCUTOR: Did you know, Mister Ghost, that marriage is an institution?

GHOST: Yes, sir, I had heard that said.

INTERLOCUTOR: Well, sir, so is an insane asylum! Did you know, Mister Ghost, that love makes the world go round? Well, sir, so does a sock in the jaw! Which reminds me, sir. An Indian from Batoche came up to me the other day and said he hadn't had a bite in days. So I bit him! Do you know, sir, how many Indians it takes to screw in a light bulb?

GHOST: What's a light bulb?

INTERLOCUTOR: Good one, Mister Ghost, a very good one. Well then, sir, if it's nighttime here, it must be winter in Regina. Nothing could be finah than Regina in the wintah, sir. Am I making myself clear? Does this bear repeating? Does this buffalo repeating? Almighty Gas, you say! Answer me, Mister Ghost. Answer! What! A fine time to demand a medium! It's very small of you, sir. I promise you I will large this in your face if you do not choose to co-operate. Tell me, is it true that the Indian brave will marry his wife's sister so he doesn't have to break in a new mother-in-law? Does it therefore follow, sir, that our good and great Queen Victoria keeps her Prince Albert in a can? That's where she keeps the Indians! Hear ye, hear ye! Don't knock off her bonnet and stick her in her royal rump with a sword, sir. The word, sir, is treason. Or are you drunk? Besotted! Be seated, sir. No! Standup! You, sir, you, I recognize you now. You're that redskin! You're that wagon burner! That feather head, Chief Bullshit. No, Chief Shitting Bull! Oh, no, no. Blood-thirsty savage. Yes, you're primitive, uncivilized, a cantankerous cannibal! Unruly redman, you lack human intelligence! Stupidly stoic, sick, demented, foaming at the maws! Weirdly mad and dangerous, alcoholic, diseased, dirty, filthy, stinking, ill-fated degenerate race, vanishing, lazy, mortifying, fierce, fierce and crazy, crazy, shit, shit, shit, shit...

GHOST: What's a light bulb?

INTERLOCUTOR: Who are you? Who the hell are you?

GHOST: I'm a dead Indian. I eat crow instead of buffalo.

INTERLOCUTOR: That's good. That's very good.

The lights shift from variety to spectral as the spotlight finds the placard: "SCENE NINE: FINALE"

INTERLOCUTOR: Who am I? Do you know?

GHOST: I recognized you by your eyes.

INTERLOCUTOR: Who am I?

GHOST: White Girl, my White Girl.

INTERLOCUTOR: Who? Who's that?

GHOST: My fierce, crazy little girl. My wife. *Ni-wiki-makan.* (my wife)...

The GHOST goes and dances in celebration to a drum. The woman removes the ... white face and costume, becoming White GIRL again. She gathers the costume in her arms as the spotlight drifts away to become a full moon in the night. White GIRL lifts a baby-sized bundle to the audience as the GHOST continues to dance in the fading lights.

My guess is that *Almighty Voice and His Wife* works like a purging or an exorcism, that the GHOST spooks the INTERLOCUTOR and the audience. It feels like it gets a lot of the poison out.

A more recent play seems to only have ghosts in its title and in the minds of the characters, doesn't go breaking through fourth walls or other conventions.

What it does do is explore the source of the poison.

The three white people in *The Moon and Dead Indians*, the first part of *The Indian Medicine Shows*, gather around a cabin in the foothills in New Mexico in 1878, barely living on the land, survivors of the frontier who are haunted by a denial of their parts in that process.

JON: Your hands are like ice. I'll go build up the fire.

MA: I heard them, Jonny.

JON: What?

MA: That's why I was afraid.

JON: Let's not talk about it, Ma.

MA: But I heard them.

JON: You didn't.

MA: Coming across the valley. You know the way sound carries. They were down in the pine bush.

JON: They wouldn't make no noise.

MA: Their horses do. They can't make their horses be sneaky.

JON: Ma, look at me.

MA: The hooves on the rocks as they crossed the brook. Knock-knock. Knock-knock. Even I could hear it.

JON: There ain't no Indians.

MA: I could hear the leather of their saddles creaking.

JON: They's all gone. All the redskins vanished.

MA: It's the sound of death coming, Jonny. You know that. You know the sound of death.

JON: Ma. Ma, look at me.

MA: What is it?

JON: They's all rounded up, Ma. Rounded up or shot.

MA: What's wrong, baby?

JON: There's no Apaches round here no more. You know that. No Apaches, no Comanches, no more God damned wild Indians!

MA: (slaps him) Don't talk to me that way!

JON: Jesus protects us, Ma.

When I was first writing *The Moon and Dead Indians* for a 24-Hour Playwrighting Contest during Nakai Theatre's White-horse Writers Festival, what happens in the play appalled me. A glib description of the crime might use the words sex, violence and racism. I couldn't believe it was coming out of me. I kept trying to comfort myself, explained the bad behaviour of the characters, the final horror of the piece by saying with some irony that it had to be because this was my first play with white characters.

But I really don't see the world like a politician.

A friend, Wayson Choy, recently published his first novel, *The Jade Peony*, and, reading it, I was reminded that the Chinese community, too, used to, maybe still do, refer to white people by words that translate as "ghosts".

And certainly the anguished characters of *The Moon and Dead Indians* are lost, souls far from their homelands, their peoples.

Would that fair-skinned, dark-haired, young man who turned away hurt and angry from the ghost drunk in *Coyote City* under-stand these characters any better? Would my Artistic Director?

White as a colour only exists because some of us get told we're black or yellow or Indians. I think my ghosts exist to probe this white problem, this tonal confusion, to spook its metaphors. Maybe my ghosts are like mirrors, but from a funhouse.

I want to spin new meanings out the stereotype or turn it into a cliché trying. Once white itself is a ghost, colour will be just a too-simple beginning of rich and strange complexities.

We'll all have tender skins.

Strange, I am, I guess, being interested all along in the pale faces and why they seem to want everyone to be as lost as they are. But it happens after a while. You end up related to some of them, and you don't want your own going off alone.

Yes, it's curious fun.

But someday, Native actors will get to play the parts in *The Moon and Dead Indians* and, unlike me, they won't even imagine needing to do it in whiteface.

(1996)

LOVING *CEREMONY*

Okay. I admit it. I love this book.

No, I don't mean I sleep with it. Not anymore.

I admit that first time I read it — here's the truth behind a cliché book cover blurb — I couldn't put it down, did end up wide awake in bed with it late into the night.

I can admit that. Hasn't everybody had that sort of at-first-sight reading experience? Maybe not. It is rare, in my life at least.

But, hey, I am jaded, a writer who reads mostly these days as part of my work, research or evaluation, or just keeping up with what's happening on the scene, literary, scientific, mythic — whatever stuff should concern a poet. It really is rare that I get or take the opportunity to read just for fun. I almost forget, sometimes, what a good read is all about.

And the fun of the good read was of course what got me started down this particular path. Reading this book again has been good for my memory, even if I did do it so I could talk to you about it, as part of the job . . .

It reminded me of what I think I'm doing, with writing as my life, beyond the business (such as it is) of writing for a living.

How do I love this book?

I can only begin to count the ways, but I'm grateful for the opportunity to do so today.

Perhaps, first of all, for its beauty, the pleasures of the rhythms of its prose, for the precision of its images.

Sentences like these about tongues are just so right: "When the corn was gone, the mule licked for the salt taste on his hand;

the tongue was rough and wet, but it was also warm and precise across his fingers." Or: "He reached into his mouth and felt his own tongue; it was dry and dead, the carcass of a tiny rodent."

But this is a beauty any reader might appreciate, that might infatuate anyone. Because how often do we get to read anymore for those simple pleasures?

And with this book, I am definitely not talking about a one-night stand. Sure, at first, it had the rush of a crush, but it's been, like, six years and here I am, still singing its praises. Yes, this is about more than killing time — what an awful phrase! Sad, that the way we live our lives today makes large parts of them expendable. We miss those experiences in art or science or religion, suspended or extended imagination, thought or faith, the cultural habits or opportunities that, through their simplicities and possibilities, remind us of, and help us to know, to define our humanity. To have the freedom to be aware, even in the ordinariness of our day by day, of what we hope we're working for.

And certainly *Ceremony* did do that (again) for me.

So, is my love for it then the love for a great work of art?

Yes, even if that, in great part, is made up of admiration, even awe. Like, wow, I wished I'd done that.

But what was it that Leslie Marmon Silko's novel *Ceremony* had done to me?

I'd had a good read. It was fun, even (well) thrilling. What does it take to thrill the jaded of this world? What the regular reader may think is "lovely" or "fun," "a good read," is not necessarily going to be lovely or fun or good for me. I admit that. What I think is thrilling, as often as not, is chilling for someone else. And there is a bit of a chill, a darkness, I admit, beating away like a drum at the heart of the novel *Ceremony*.

It's funny/strange. When invited to do this talk, *Ceremony* was my first thought. But the funny/strange thing was that I did not really remember the book as a whole. Oh sure, I remembered the arc of the thing, the story of the mixed-up soldier (mixed up in blood, in culture) returning from the war, of his journey toward balance.

But I'd forgotten so many of the details. Like the lovely, non-clinical description of the soldier, Tayo's, state of mind:

> . . . how the world had come undone, how thousands of miles, high ocean waves and green jungles could not hold people in their place. Years and months had become weak, and people could push against them and wander back and forth in time. Maybe it had always been this way and he was only seeing it for the first time.

Not only did it seem to me to be about a mind in crisis — is this what they call "a fugue state?" — I thought it also could serve as a description of the world the mind knows before it's trained to the time clocks make, and the space outlined by maps. Uncivilized or prehistoric or even childlike. And the discovery (again in the story) that old calendars served as part of the medicine man's paraphernalia, this time through, made a perfect childlike sort of sense to me.

But then, coming again upon the page with the star map was truly a shock. I'd forgotten all about it.

As I had the story of Helen Jean. Where did this come from?

And I was amazed that Tayo's liaison with the woman with the ochre eyes totally slipped my mind.

Hey, there's not a lot of sex in this book. You'd think it would stick. I guess we all get old.

But what I had remembered most clearly, what had come back to me in the instant when I thought of *Ceremony*, was the thrilling dark story, almost a legend there just beyond the book's midpoint, the story that's told about witches and the causation of white people. I guess, despite its darkness, I want to call it a creation story.

There are at least two things about that story that made it important to me.

The first was aesthetic. Around the time I first came upon this book I'd been mulling over a lot of ideas around form and function in my art, at least as far as it's vaguely expressed in the words "writing" and "telling." This arose from the realization that oral literature ("orature" as one of my friends puts it), that apparent subset of world literature, had been reserved in these parts as Native territory. And I'd been quite taken by the possibility of identifying as a storyteller. That identity felt more like what I was interested in exploring as part of my shifty self than did the identity of writer.

I mean hey, doesn't "the writer" write novels and articles for publishers and magazines and newspapers and get paid a lot for it? Okay, a lot only relative to what I was, what I still do get paid, persistently doing poetry and (to add perversely to my unmarketableness) plays, so maybe I thought by claiming the label "storyteller," I might rationalize these uneconomic habits or behaviours.

And I'd started drifting toward silly but still, somehow, dramatic generalities — hey, I am a playwright, I've a developed instinct for contradiction — silly generalities like white people write prose on white pages and Native people tell stories to the open ear, generalities like prose is the dead language of the soul, sold like meat in stores, while storytelling is a living body, social, sexy, a performance, yeah, you can't catch me.

Yes, this is what artists sometimes do — create their own brands of anguish out of aesthetic gobbledygook! The artistic version of the mid-life crisis — though it doesn't only happen then.

But then *Ceremony* appeared with both writing and storytelling in it, both representation and presentation, and the sequences were working in tandem, making a storytelling rich with all the strengths of both of what I'd supposed were opposed aesthetics, a perfect example, Native consensus, compromise, the Native tradition of adapting, of creating anew traditions.

This really practical solution to my conundrum helped me out of the gobbledygook, let me get down to work with more of a sense that I did and do know what I'm doing.

This did nothing for my marketableness.

Still, my love brought me assurance, comfort, healing.

And even though I still do prefer the oral art forms, I spend less time looking for rationalizations.

The second thing about that story that made it so memorable was, I guess, also partly aesthetic, but mostly either political or mythical. Maybe it was both.

This story, by taking the different tact, telling a different myth about the beginnings of history on this continent, by retelling the story usually told as the coming of the white man and the destruction of the red as a dark comedy of active evil, changed the sense, the mythic meaning of the conditions I/we Native people find ourselves in here, from tragic to epic, from a story of victims — a story repeated endlessly everywhere we look, and isn't it boring? — to a story of human struggling beings.

I was probably also thrilled a little bit perversely by the fact that the new story pulled the rug out from under the Man and turned him into a pawn of forces greater than he, for a change, could understand. (See how you guys like it.)

A story changing my mind, turning it around, that to me too is lovely.

But this was not entirely a new experience for me.

Sure, it is the sort of thing that thrills the jaded professional but, as part of my aesthetic practice, I'm always on the lookout for a new way to tell a story, a different point of view on a narrative, the narrative that defines reality.

It's the creator's practice of relativity.

And I'm also always on the lookout for a new story, despite what literary critics always say in their universalistic mood, about there only being so many stories in the world. A dozen or twenty-seven.

Whatever.

They don't encourage those of us who write to do more than the job of the jazzman, playing variations on recognized themes.

But I live in hope of new stories anyway.

The traditional way of seeing stories as models of society, of how we live our lives, begs the question of how we will grow old together successfully if we don't get those new stories, stories with more of all of us really in them.

Here, in North America at least, the dilemma I feel is that society at large seems to accept stories mainly as product and/or entertainment.

But imagine if stories, like in the good old days or our childhoods, did have morals, we might think:

I never heard that one before!

Really?

They believe that?

Maybe we could too . . .

Think with excitement.

Yes, I listen hopefully.

And my hope was rewarded by this story.

And the way that dark creation story functioned in the novel as part parallel, part guide to the soldier's story reassured me that my own ways of working, when my own stories are often inspired, informed by old ones, was worth taking seriously.

I admit, often I wonder if I'm not just goofing around, I'm having so much fun when the work's going well. And this dilemma is especially persistent for any writer who works at plays!

But here was this scary, thrilling story. And a great part of its moral had to be about retaking control of our destinies.

Talk about empowering. No wonder I'd love it.

Wouldn't you? Well, maybe not.

I'm not one of those artists who thinks the great work of art necessarily expresses universals, ideas or ideals that everyone shares. I'm — I admit it — a bit more of a democrat than that, suspect that in a democracy what matters and is most interesting are our differences.

Hey, there's no accounting for taste.

And we do all have differing tastes in our admittedly multicultural society.

And I assume what science tells us about our sameness, that we're right down there, swimming around together in the same (so to speak) gene pool. We're essentially the same — deoxyribonucleic acids. So shouldn't it be a shame not to celebrate our differences?

And (to parse the worn but wise cliché) isn't variety the spice?

Sure, I might/maybe saying this because I am apparently different, other, a member by fate, tendency, history and (yes) decision of a number of special interest groups as defined by racist Canadian law and economic history, culture and custom — Yes, I might/maybe doing here the sort of thing that's been derided as special pleading, but hey, just how important are aesthetic concerns in the political scheme of things in this part of the world?

And isn't it part of the dilemma of those politics that we in the Native community are special? That's what the label First Nation was created to pin down. I'm not about to be treated (say) like Rushdie for exploring these alternatives, now am I?

Why do I even feel the need to ask the rhetorical question?

Yes, a great work of art may very well contain some universal wisdom, some such thought, and certainly in the distance of time and utility we can see that some of (say) Shakespeare or Van Gogh, Hitchcock or the Beatles, still do have something to do with our current and/or continuing fears and desires.

Sure.

But as a working artist, the effort to be universal has to be the least of my concerns.

And I have to trust other wisdom, thoughts I've received from my teachers and fellows — and from my own experience — wisdom that's too usually expressed as "Write about what you know" but is also connected to that bit of artistic faith that says that by being particular one will thus express the universal. Was it Blake's phrase — "the Universe in a grain of sand?" Yes, I have to express my own particular — possibly peculiar — grain of sand as clearly as I can, even if it means occasionally getting a little grating in the shells of my own and other's ears, although usually I prefer something smoother.

Like I think Leslie Silko's managed in *Ceremony*. She just slipped it right in so delicately.

> He had believed that on certain nights, when the moon rose full and wide as a corner of the sky, a person standing on the high sandstone cliff of that mesa could reach the moon. Distances and days existed in themselves then; they all had a story. They were not barriers. If a person wanted to get to the moon, there was a way; it all depended on whether you knew the directions — exactly which way to go and what to do to get there; it depended on whether you knew the story of how others before you had gone. He had believed in the stories for a long time, until the teachers at Indian school taught him not to believe in that kind of "nonsense."

There's more than a hint of another model of the world there. As there is in:

> The word he chose to express "fragile" was filled with the intricacies of a continuing process, and with a strength

inherent in spider webs woven across paths through sand hills where early in the morning the sun becomes entangled in each filament of web. It took a long time to explain the fragility and intricacy because no word exists alone, and the reason for choosing each word had to be explained with a story about why it must be said this certain way. That was the responsibility that went with being human, old Ku'oosh said, the story behind each word must be told so there could be no mistake in the meaning of what had been said; and this demanded great patience and love.

And there may also be an explanation of the art of storytelling there as well. And where else would you learn things like that?

I mean, one of the other bits of wisdom I've received hanging out with other Native artists and reading Native writers is that traditionally, the story the storyteller told served three functions.

Here I interject that, yes, this is a large generalization, probably an oversimplification, when you consider how many hundreds of different Native cultures existed before Columbus. But think of it rather as a small thought, a fragment of wisdom, all we've got left after everything that happened in the five hundred and counting years since so-called history came to the Americas.

Could I suggest that stories with such social functions are acknowledged characteristics of any society prior to the modern or post-modern one we find ourselves in? Which is only to say that, though we don't always acknowledge them today, we're so (post) modern, I think they're still doing their jobs.

Reconsider the word "prehistoric," and try to get past our prejudices about what it means as far as the so-calleds of "progress" and "sophistication" go. Technologically we may be progressing, growing more complex and complicated by the day. But socially we seem to be headed the other way.

Our Native traditions say the three functions of all stories pre-historically seem to have been: (1) to entertain, (2) to instruct, and (3) to heal. There doesn't seem to me to be much to argue with in that.

And I, at least, in *Ceremony* found pleasure, learning and emotional reassurance. What more could I want?

It's a great book.

And such results — pleasure, learning, emotional reassurance — make the practice of art sound like a really responsible thing to do, a service to your fellows, even (say) a vocation of a sort.

As I've learned and like to tell my students, a path with honour.

No wonder a writer like Silko is concerned with ceremonies — which do the same things.

Of course, this only begins to explore my own particular, maybe peculiar love of this book, but I want to make use of my last few minutes to look at something it seems I hate and, in the process, I hope to suggest why you might not have heard tell before of such a great writer as Leslie Marmon Silko.

Consider how strange it is that a lot of writers shy away from claiming to teach anybody anything, don't want to be accused of preaching, and with modesty (apparently) would never claim healing as among their powers or duties. They leave that stuff to the professionals, to teachers and leaders and doctors.

Medicine means different things in our different cultures. Other writers, of course, do claim to have something to say and we all know which way we turn when we see them coming.

Unless, like (say) Shaw, they're impossibly entertaining. How modern or post, the specialization that rips the three functions apart.

(Maybe the new downsized art that results from these days of decreased funding will put them back together and writers like Silko could rise back into fashion?)

One wonders about those artists, what it was about their own educations or religious upbringings that they are so averse to being thought to inhabit even something close to the same territory.

Oh, I admit I wouldn't want to get caught trying to teach or preach.

No, I wouldn't want to get caught.

I always say "I got through school," as if, on certain levels, it was a struggle against my will.

And I joke that "My parents dragged me to church" — usually when they can hear me.

All this was done for my own good, but the end result is an experience of education and religion as brainwashing, as an abuse of power over the kid I once was.

Socialization as trauma, I guess.

So maybe other artists, writers looking for an audience or just looking for their own healing, looking for their own human freedom, in much the same reflex, turn away from anything having to do with instruction or the wisdom of the past.

Oh, we've progressed far beyond all that, they say.

But what do they have left? Can't you hear them aggressively claiming: "It's just a story." "It's just entertainment." "Art for art's sake." "It don't mean nothing."

Doesn't this all seem rather disingenuous?

Can they really be so dismissive of their own life's work?

And, of course, the worse of these (I'm being so bold to bitch, here's where the hate comes in) is "art for art's sake."

Which has only been on the list of functions of art, if function it is, since — I don't know, Oscar Wilde? And when one looks at his own fables, any of his stories, and sees that they have moral points, that they do in fact teach — well, disingenuous, yes.

But the result is all the modern, post-modern, academic talk about style, abstraction, signifiers, all the blather, usually translated from the French.

Pardon my French.

Look at any work of abstract expression and once you get past the formal, infantile delights of colour and balance and texture, stuff any kid does in kindergarten, what's left?

Fear. Of. Content.

Neurotic art?

Fear of history, of story.

No healing there.

No wonder we wonder about the psyches and sex lives of famous painters. No grownup worries here about having to heal or educate or entertain, no siree. Just a complex desire for uncomplicated pleasure. And I do mean "complex." Did Freud list this one? Does it go along with the fetishes?

Or is this what's meant by the phrase "classic passive-aggressive?"

So, is fine art today largely regressing toward childhood and self-containment, no longer a spiritual practice but a technical one, no longer maintaining many connections with the knowledges of religion or science?

Can it be so smug?

But hey, I guess there is nothing wrong with masturbation.

Didn't Woody Allen claim to be a great lover because he practised a lot at home by himself?

So now, of course, art free of teaching and healing is being forced into making connections with commerce, but that's another lecture . . .

You might understand why I find Silko and her *Ceremony* so worthy. Just in contrast.

And there really is so little literature by or about Native people around, or so little that can be easily found, and even less that makes its way across those recently drawn lines called international borders, that those of us who identify ourselves that way, as Native, or who are just interested in this part of the world, its history, its people, who we are beyond the tunnel visions of scientists or politicians or the more simply ignorant, well, we're always more than hungry for any bit of Native literature we can get our hands on.

So it seems, in that context, that the fashion for art that neither teaches nor heals and barely entertains and, therefore, excludes the stuff that does as old-fashioned, unsophisticated, primitive et cetera, ends up feeling like just another part of the — what's the political phrase? — racist hegemony.

Hey, it's another one of those different points of view I'm always on the lookout for.

And it's probably too simple a point of view to retell any story from with sufficient richness to manage to heal anyone's hate.

But lucky me, with my copy of Leslie Silko's *Ceremony*.

When I picked the book up from that half-price book bin outside of the Reader's Den up on Bloor Street, on what I remember now as a bright spring day, I thought I was doing it out of my sense of duty mostly and curiosity leastwise, just doing my job, and all at a bargain for a mere five bucks.

But I don't know what the day was really like, and think I only remember it now as a bright day, a warm day, sunny like spring, simply because, like spring often does, it brought me something I could fall in love with.

(1996)

A BRIDGE ACROSS TIME

About Ben Cardinal's
Generic Warriors and
No Name Indians

I am thinking of a landscape just north of Saskatoon as I start thinking about Ben Cardinal's play *Generic Warriors and No Name Indians*. I am thinking about Waneskewin, the traditional culture centre there, a place I have been privileged to visit only once. I am dwelling again on that valley because it seems just the sort of place the characters in Cardinal's play inhabit.

I'm remembering my own November day there, the wind and a bright cold sky overhead. I recall making my way alone along a sheltered path among the bare willows on the riverbank, my street shoes slipping or printing tracks in the fresh half-inch of snow. Had ice begun to grow out from the shore despite the current? The water still had a dark look to it. In that valley below those rounded slopes, there were few other people I met and acknowledged with waves or nods in my hour-long walk. Those people and myself were the only evidence of the modern world.

If I had been like Cardinal's contemporary Native family in their house beside such a river, with their music and guns, their word processor and misunderstandings, in the shadow of a railroad trestle, in the eddies of the wind, it might have been simpler for me to begin imagining a meeting around the next bend in the path with an ancestor still alive, a warrior from the Battle of Batoche — the battlefield not that far along the South Saskatchewan — or his wife cooking over a smokeless fire.

But I was a visitor there, almost a city slicker, and not until at last, breath short and cheeks glowing with the effort, I climbed up the slope to the prairie, climbed into the wind, and found myself looking over a medicine wheel did I clearly feel or imagine in the light, the cold, the distances, the power of the place. It felt open and eternal, somehow a place outside of time, the essence of possibilities.

And all I had done to get there was to follow that river.

Perhaps I ought to try to explain it away and say that obviously I was able to feel that way, in part, because I had already passed sites where the archeological evidence of ancient villages and a buffalo jump were slowly coming to the surface.

Perhaps it is true that because I'd been reassured, thanks to science, that people had inhabited that place for immeasurable times before our current version of history had begun that I was able to respond in that less than straightforward, less than scientific way.

But I was also able to imagine that way in part because I felt like those prehistoric people were family, not only the ancestors of Cardinal's Musk and Mabel, but my own predecessors. I imagine this way not only because, as they say, I identify as a Native person — usually when "they" are trying to bully me into admitting the overly simple, white-washed identity of Canadian — but more immediately because I still had the memory of *Generic Warriors and No Name Indians* in my head.

Seeing the play, even in my far part of the country, in the city, those how many years before, had prepared me for that *déja vu* sort of day when I was actually *in situ* by that river. It had introduced me not only to specific human characters in its foreground but had also given me an abiding sense, if not necessarily a clear picture, of the characteristics of its literal background. I was ready to meet that place when I arrived because I had already visited there, thanks to Mr. Cardinal.

Those many years before, I had felt no need to be introduced to Musk and Mabel, Florence and Sarah, the family the play centres on. Them I recognized immediately, the type of raw comic characters they were.

Yes, I knew about the struggle of the men, Musk and Ennis, to be warriors, whatever that means in times of defeat or peace like ours. And I thought I could pretty well predict the course of the impatient love of a woman like Mabel. And there, through Florence and Sarah, was ye olde generation gap gaping as the times dictate.

Oh, I thought I knew the heart of this play, thought it was a mere comedy about a family in crisis.

I had not at first been aware of the obvious, the unmentioned landscape, which so often falls into the realm of the untouched, if not intangible, in plays.

Most plays are only about people, about characters. So I had no idea that this family's crisis could be located and focused into possibilities for the personal, the poetic, the political, the spiritual, for common sense, by a railway bridge crossing a river. In Ben Cardinal's *Generic Warriors and No Name Indians*, the landscape is also a character, the *deus in machina*.

It starts with a river in Saskatchewan crossed by a railroad bridge. What better place to begin talking about a meeting of eternity and history, about natural cycles and progress, about families and warriors?

I suppose my first clue that something more was going on should have been the grand entry across the bridge that erupts out of nowhere (or "sometime?") at the top of the play, but at first I just took it for a theatrical gesture. This seemed a fair enough assumption in a world where powwow so often seems to mean a big show and most plays are just about characters.

A series of historically and geographically separate scenes took me well into the play. I met the family alive in the here and now of 1990, the soldier Floyd and his "consort" Marlena in Europe in 1944, and finally the warrior Muskwa and his wife Pihew in the here of 1885 and, following that, again earlier that year, as if, confusingly, their story was curling back on itself, an eddy between the current and the shore of a river.

(This confusing eddying, spiralling of the narrative will happen again in the love story of Floyd and Marlena.)

Only then, when the next scene back in 1990 reintroduced me to the character Floyd, did I start to clue in. Musk in 1990 had already told me the man was dead, but here he is in 1990, loud and lively, and funny, lounging on the tracks, talking to his buddy Ennis. He looks old as Ennis, seems hard of hearing — or is it an act like the one my Grandad used to put on for dealing with my Grandma? I laughed. He's a veteran you would recognize in any Branch of the Canadian Legion that let Indians in. (That injustice, exclusion from the society of warriors, is one he and Ennis do suffer in the now.) You have to shout as if he's a long way off, even when he's right beside you.

And while Floyd is certainly at home in Saskatchewan, he is also out of place, out of time, in the now. How to explain this? The simple answer is that he is only Ennis' drunken hallucination, which would make Ennis a pathetic survivor of the War.

But this play is not only about Ennis and his psychology — Cardinal is not very interested in the study of individual psychology: his focus seems to be family and community — so a more complex answer, and something more suitable to a comedy, is necessary. What if he's a ghost, a ghost as haunted by his memories of the War as Ennis is by him?

But before long it becomes clear that he is even more than a ghost, that he has a reality in the play separate from haunting. He is able to be a young man at any moment and to go running off into the past, more easily than Ennis is able to remember it. For him, the past is not some distant land left behind in the flow of time. It seems no more distant than the far side of the river.

The character Floyd, appearing on the bridge at a moment where a hand-held lantern is substituted for the headlight of an onrushing locomotive, a theatrical sleight of hand, was himself a bridge across time.

The landscape of *Generic Warriors and No Name Indians* is one ripe with possibility, with history, or histories, one full of stories not only of this one family stretched out across time but also of characters from sacred tales, like Weesageechak. It is a place in which one character's fiction is another's truth — what Sarah thought was just her "story" is the reality of Muskwa and Pihew. It is a stage where the distortions of memory and desire can find true expression in the reprise of a musical number. It is a location where every time seems to exist in familiar proximity. It is the cosmos where an eclipse of the male sun by the female moon is an expression of the possibility of harmony. It is a dream constructed in a way that functions like personal memory or nightmare — pratfalls hard on the images of bloodletting.

It is a reality that pushes theatre toward cinema with the cutting speed it uses to shift scenes. It has almost no taste, but a lot of laughs.

Is it the eternal present tense, surreal, comic, mysterious?

Those many years ago, back in the city, when I had first seen the play, I had found all its qualities both confusing and exhilarating, and finally touching. I had not recognized what it was about, but I had felt so excited by it, it had seemed the best play I had seen that theatre season.

At Waneskewin, to talk to Saskatchewan writers about some ideas I had been playing with about how Native writers write differently from non-Native writers, I saw the reason I have fallen in love with the play had to do with recognizing the way it structured reality and the landscape that reality grew from.

As I said, the grand entry that erupts out of nowhere at the top of the play should have been my first clue to understanding the play. I should have known because the talk I was about to give began by considering the image of a grand entry at a powwow, that great circling and spiralling in of dancers, as a ceremonial, artistic expression of family and community, and a celebration of life's non-linearity.

The landscape of this epic comedy *Generic Warriors and No Name Indians* seems to me most comprehensible if we keep those possibilities of the spiral in mind. Out there in the wind, the light, the distances of the prairies, time is no longer the straight and narrow line demanded by the progress of history or the history of progress. It is a spiral that contains the centre of the world, the eternal moment where each of us lives.

From their places, their moments on that spiral, a character like Floyd or a writer like Ben Cardinal can look sideways and find the freedom to escape history and the injustices of the moment, can embrace the members of their family and communities, despite their displacement through eternity.

From that spiral, we can look back at our lives with enough wisdom to love them.

That medicine wheel in Waneskewin made it clear to me just how grand an entry into the theatre *Generic Warriors and No Name Indians* was.

(1997)

FLAMING NATIVITY

About Billy Merasty's Fireweed

So have you heard the one about the faggot Indian?

Maybe I should have said "the Indian faggot."

Oh, whichever epithet I might choose to use hardly makes much difference. Your answer is most likely "No." Hey, why use two, both sticks and stones, why overdo it, when either one would be sufficient to the put-down? Yeah, either one has always been enough to build a good story around.

Until now, of course, when some of them Indians have begun to ram this damn political — or is it historical or cultural? — correctness down our throats.

Why can't they take a joke? Hell, talk about doing Calijah.

"First Nations?" Just what is the story there? It sounds like a brand of diapers. Native renaissance, my ass. On second thought, never mind my ass.

"Hey, have you heard the one about the First Nation faggot?" just doesn't work. Oh joke, where is thy sting?

And — wouldn't you know it? — now they're starting to reassert stories about their national identities. It was so much simpler when they all were just Indians. Hey,, you can't live in the past. We're supposed to be able to tell that there's something different between that Cree and this Delaware or whatever? Aren't we all just Canadians?

Who's doing the coyote calls?

And now that they're rediscovering their traditional cultures, some of them are actually trying to do away with that old and trusty set of insults, faggot, fairy, queer, sissy — even the kids can use them! — and replace them with this New Age-y sounding "two-spirited" thing. I mean, talk about lisp-wristed. Aren't Indians supposed to be warriors? Real men? That's the story I'm used to hearing.

And what about their morals? They do not to seem to give an American plug nickel that the Judaeo-Christian God might not like this threat to the fertility of the tribe. Yeah, strangely enough, it seems like their Gitchy Manitou, their Great Mystery, actually made some people queer so they could serve, in the interest of harmony, as intermediaries between the divisions of the world, women and men, life and death — us and Ottawa maybe.

What next? Jesus and all the apostles notwithstanding, if this keeps up, "gay" is going to start sounding really normal. Oh for the days of yore when it was just something Christmassy, whenever that was . . .

"Have you heard the one about the two-spirited Cree?" just isn't funny.

So what about this *Fireweed* play by William (Billy) Merasty? What about its cutely ironic subtitle "An Indigeni Fairy Tale"?

Well, okay, okay, if we are to believe what it says, maybe I should have said "Have you heard the one about the two-spirited Cree? It isn't *just* funny." It's also glamorous in the original sense, charming our imaginations with actual magic tricks as well as a full hand of more usual theatrics — fire, light and lightning, sound, character, stories and their telling.

Its central story of a journey toward healing and home is also a story about escaping that dark side of glamour, the curse, which is laid down in this particular plot by, of course, a man in black, a priest. We would be offended by this pitiful church bashing if we were not also being teased by this twist on the usual fairy tale, this seemingly new or at least naughty and possibly even feminist (Who knew Native culture would have to do with women too?) point of view — although if we are to trust the teller, it is an ancient way of seeing. No wonder, despite all the anguish of the story's journey, it remains seductive, mysterious, erotic.

Which is of course why, though *Fireweed* may be the first one we here have heard tell of these doubly epitheted individuals, faggot Indians, Indian faggots, it is certainly not going to be the last. Who knew we could get into such bent and effeminate territory by following this Native renaissance movement? Who knew a Native nativity might involve more than feathered headdresses and war paint, and how, yes, how the Hiawatha did they keep quiet about it for so long?

How the heart of Merasty's *Fireweed* aches for lost loves, for suicides and those who are taught by the church to hate themselves, the queers and the Indians. But then it remembers how heartbeats go on.

Its central character, Peechweechum Rainbowshield, referred to hereafter as Rainbow, thrown into a holding cell in nothing but his underwear, insulted and assaulted by a police officer, somehow pulls a little red dress, lipstick and high heels out of nowhere. The beautiful young man proceeds to do a drag musical number as his version of the great escape act, disappearing, the vanishing Indian, from that Winnipeg jail into the dream stream of the play.

He slips through the iron bars and stones of the white man's law and religion and right into his and our community's mythology, much the same way his predecessor, the legendary medicine dreamer, Isiah Iskootee'oo, did in the long ago to the frustration of the Royal Canadian Mounted Police. Isiah Iskootee'oo escaped punishment, the story goes, for setting fire to the bush, destroying Her Majesty's timber. But now that we have recovered the knowledge — the Native renaissance again — that burning was used traditionally to manage forest environments and facilitate hunting, Isiah Iskootee'oo's misdemeanour appears in a more heroic light.

So the scene in *Fireweed* where Rainbow escapes, theatrically, magically, perhaps — yes — perhaps incredibly (it is early in the renaissance after all), from laws that would punish him for a crime called "Gross Indecency" may just be a first and teasing glimpse of recovered knowledge, an alternative mythology and some common sense about sexual behaviour.

The scene is certainly pivotal to the play, erupting spontaneous theatrical combustion, burning down the fourth wall, allowing the character Rainbow to step out of the narrative, as well as his cell, and play with and to us in the audience, just like the characters of the Flight Attendant or Reena Lightningway or even the Judge who are all spirits and not limited by flesh and blood bodies or dramaturgical realities.

Fireweed, before this scene, is a story about Rainbow, a young man haunted and made almost hopeless by the suicide of his beloved twin brother in the inferno of a burning church. He is haunted by the possibility that he, a medicine-minded young Cree, as the object not only of his rather Catholic brother's love but of his sexual desire, may have been the cause of a great sin — is the dilemma faith or homosexuality or incest, or all the above? He fears he may have been the cause of his brother's suicide.

This spiritual murkiness is lit only by the presence of the above mentioned guardian spirits (the "fairy god parents" the play's ironic subtitle invokes) and the Manitoba Legislature's Golden Boy, emblem here of the possibility of love. The play suggests a version of Winnipeg that is a sort of hell on earth, streets where sex, drugs, and rock and roll are never expressions of growth, exploration, joy and youth, but always mean meaningless, directionless despair.

Rainbow's little red dress number redresses this. After its performance, like magic, the story, the stories *Fireweed* tells take on a motive, become hopeful, helpful, loving, and shift Rainbow toward reconciliation with his two-spirited self and his family (his most Catholic mother) and his community (his auntish medicine teacher). He is saved at the same time his former lover Raven is lost. It may be that because Rainbow is able to accept and express, even so campily, his own female spirit that he finds his way home.

Rainbow's little red dress number acts like a front door into a strangely familiar house, a dream world, a memory of adolescence when the erotic was more than the body, was what the whole world was about. The drag number is itself the essence of queer, two-spirited, both true and false, male and female, and is the play's intermediary between us (the audience) and them, our forgotten desires, our bodies.

The home Rainbow returns to is a place not only of pristine wilderness but also of ancient stories, a mythology that is a way to wisdom about our lives, about the body and its hungers. No wonder Rainbow needs to hear again the ones about Weesageechak, the Cree trickster, needs to relive one of that great spirit's adventures.

The Weetigo, that embodiment of morbid hunger, traps and threatens to eat Weesageechak, as western civilization does with Indians. Only Weesageechak's own cunning and the help of a weasel, who is willing to journey into the Weetigo's body, via its anus and inners, allows Weesageechak to survive — and the weasel to be beautiful. What more visceral, funny, and queer representation of a journey into and through our fears or lives could we ask for?

Hey, shit happens.

Have you heard the one about the Indian faggot and Weesageechak and the Weetigo? Yeah. It proves things have a way of working out in the end.

(1997)

OF THE ESSENCE

About Tomson Highway's
The Sage, the Dancer
and the Fool

I remember being bothered, both puzzled and exhilarated, the first time I saw Tomson Highway's stage poem *The Sage, the Dancer and the Fool*.

Probably I was puzzled because it was only 1983 — if Tomson's dates are right — and I was still in recovery from my education. I was writing poetry but for some reason felt unready to deal with the plays I had in mind. I had learned a lot of things while earning a couple of degrees, one of the most useful of which for an apprentice playwright, one might have thought, should have been some clarity around what makes a play. But one of my unyielding dilemmas, as the detritus of those school years fell aside, making way for art in the so-called real world, was that the only thing I remembered from my education with any definition around the subject of plays was an often repeated credo that the only characteristic essential to a play was conflict. I know I remembered this credo of conflict to the exclusion of a lot of other ideas because it had been one of the most difficult ideas I had tried to get through my thick skull during the whole of my academic career and finally, I must admit, I did not succeed.

Years later, I realized my thickness at the time had a lot to do with growing up in the subculture of my family on the Six Nations lands, a partially Christianized, but definitely Iroquoian community, where the only activities in which conflict seemed to be permissible, let alone essential, were hockey and lacrosse, neither of which concerned me. I don't remember that the rules for social behaviour were ever actually articulated then, although there are days now when the idea of a book of aboriginal etiquette, especially focused on cross-national differences, does not seem like a bad idea. (It may be that some part of largely Iroquoian me looked at *The Sage, the Dancer and the Fool* and wondered "Just what are those Cree going on about now?") Those days I grew up in, conflicts arising in areas of our community life outside the arena were not encouraged, were seen, I suppose, as evidence of immaturity, rudeness, or a failure of imagination, if not exactly immorality. We are, of course, talking about public behaviour here. What could be more public, if you want to give your life to it, than art?

I was forced, since I wanted to write plays, to come up with another way of looking at that so-called essential characteristic of conflict, a way that might allow me with some clarity to proceed along my chosen path. So let us say that I decided, without knowing it, that my teachers, in an effort to be reasonable within the limits of their own ruling subcultures — they were professors at universities, after all — must all be making the same simple error. They were trying to turn the characteristic of conflict into a universal quality, something they already knew they valued in the structures of their legislatures (calling it debate), in their economic systems (calling it competition), in their religions ("Onward Christian Soldiers!"), and in their institution (calling it the tenure committee). It only made sense of their world to assume the characteristic of conflict in — or to impose it on — art. It just had to be one of the universals.

Of course, as I realized eventually from my discomfort, where I was coming from, it wasn't one of the universals. Essential conflict made no sense to me. It just seemed wrong. And later, as I looked around for explanations and examples, I realized that conflict was common in the dramatic literature but no more essential to any particular successful piece of theatre than, say, characters with Freudian psychology, hit songs, or a smoke machine.

I also later realized that the common sort of conflict I had been taught to recognize was as easy, as interesting and as ritualized as hockey or lacrosse. Yes, to a certain extent, it was a matter of taste, which should be more than the mouth, or why else were we being taught about art?

Yes, I was forced, since I wanted to write plays for my own interest — from my own ethnocentricity even, I'd now admit — to come up with another concept to try to pin down and maybe even understand that characteristic of a good dramatic work that caught the attention, suspended disbelief, and got the imagination going. Was it a tension? Texture? Rhythm? Some sort of suspense? Mystery? Activity? Yes.

I borrowed from what little I knew of the visual arts (I had taken a course in photography at an earlier point in my university studies, spending hours in a dark room making light from blacks and greys) the concept of "contrast." I inserted the word into the credo — "The only characteristic essential to a play is contrast" — and felt suddenly at ease. And this minor adjustment to my vocabulary allowed me to proceed with my own work, even though I had to admit, and kept expecting, that the majority of theatrical work would be informed, or even deformed, by, or in contrast to the academic conflict model. I had, after all, been taught a certain standard of taste.

So what puzzled me about *The Sage, the Dancer and the Fool*, despite my own awkward inner struggle, was that it wasn't to my educated taste, didn't illustrate the credo. Where was the conflict? What was the subject, as defined by the conflict? What was I to make of it? The piece seemed more like a poem, an exploration, a meditation, than an argument or battle. Shouldn't the obliqueness of the dilemma of being a stranger in a strange city be abandoned for the directness of good old conflict? Was this contrast between an urban now and a wilderness then and the longing that expressed sufficient to build a successful piece of theatre on?

Well, yes — because, as I've said, part of my bother with the piece was that I was also exhilarated by it.

It was an uncommonly rich theatrical experience in the Toronto of 1983, as I remember it. There were a lot of what I had come to refer to as "furniture plays" being produced, even by those venues that prided themselves on being forward looking, politically and/or aesthetically. I remember being offended that the set of one of these plays was actually applauded, audience members being pleased that it looked "so real" in a photographic reproduction sort of way. I felt sorry for the actors being forced to compete with the design. I don't remember the play at all now, the set was so outstanding, and I have to suspect that that set's connection to whatever play it was supposed to be serving was simply wrong. It now seems like those plays and those audiences were trapped in the then television version of naturalism and that their entrapment was not really allowing them that theatrical universal, the suspension of disbelief.

The Sage, the Dancer and the Fool starts out with a set that is not naturalistic at all, starts out with the assumption that the members of the audience have imaginations and want to use them. It then uses a grand piano, that rather archetypical instrument, to create a seductive, sensual music track, and gelatined lights to show the way, and sends the audience off with a Cree man, abstracted into three archetypes representing his intellect, his spirit and his body (Tomson played the intellect, his nephew Billy Merasty the spirit, and Tomson's brother Rene, the modern dancer, the body), to explore the city of Toronto as it appears only through the abstractions of colour, shadow, music, movement, and the words of both English and Cree, also often used as abstractly, as expressionistically as music. So Toronto, the city, is not defined by one "naturalistic" set but is evoked in ways as various as the realities each member of the audience imagines.

This abstract quality, which one is not surprised to find in the work of either a "much lapsed pianist" or a modern dancer when one considers it, surprised me then, because it was not what I had learned to expect, either from the theatre I could afford to attend in 1983 or from school. I may have been taught about such things, had vague memories of being told the roots of the theatre were in ritual performance, in symbolic movement, that such abstraction was, itself, theatrical, may even have explained to myself my childhood Christian fervour as a response to the Anglican ceremonial version of such abstraction, but as I have related, it wasn't what got my attention. So that night I first saw *The Sage, the Dancer and the Fool,* it either taught or reminded me — that's what the bother was about — that abstraction may well be an essential quality of a play.

It allowed us to see clearly what the play was about. It removed the extraneous particulars; the remainder was evocative. The contrast of the wealth, the torrent of urban detail the play presents, even inundates the audience with, the contrast of all those shoes, office workers, food and lights, with the simplicity of memories of a life on the land, only deepens the longing, the nostalgia, the energetic confusion *The Sage, the Dancer and the Fool* expresses. It is this emotional reality, existing, so to speak, between the lines, in the contrast between the elements of the play, that was Tomson's — and Rene's — theatrical accomplishment.

As I have suggested, in the theatrical ecology of Toronto of 1983, and even again in 1989, *The Sage, the Dancer and the Fool* stood out because of this quality. The play, I believe, even got some Dora nominations. At moments then and now, the eccentric ethnocentric in me is tempted to allow, as a lot of people assumed at the time, that this standout quality, and not its authors or its content or its point of view, was what made the play a Native play. They seemed to be looking for ways to explain away their exhilaration, to keep the Indian "other." But, of course, such abstraction is a quality of any good art. Even photography, when it reaches for art, tries to represent reality with selected, evocative detail — which is why black-and-white photographs are still, or even more beautiful, in contrast to mundane, naturalistic colour.

And that abstraction is also why *The Sage, the Dancer and the Fool* could go beyond the audience's prejudices about Indians to engage their hearts in Highways' love for our land.

(1997)

QUEER FOR A DAY

Writing the Status Queer:
Reading Beyond Breeding

One of my memories of the Writing Thru "Race" Conference is hearing someone note just after the event that the one session titled "Race and Sexuality" ended up being about homosexuality — since only gay people attended it.

This was okay with me — dare I say with most of us — since we got to have our own little queer caucus in the middle of the conference where we didn't have to guess anymore about who was or wasn't.

I suppose that little queer caucus was a bit of a breakthrough, too, for a Writers' Union event, though for me, with a variety of aboriginal arts and writing conferences under my belt, it felt only natural, although I suppose I should say cultural.

And hey, we didn't have to worry for the moment about incurring the wrath or irritation of our peers by our being so out and contrary.

There was joy as well as safety in numbers that day.

And who knows, maybe the straight people were off in a caucus of their own where they dealt with the ways racism and sexism and capitalism — oh, the whole hegemonic ball — was queering their heterosexuality up.

Did anyone receive their report?

Here today, on this panel at least, it appears there's a similar situation. All the pigmentationally challenged queers must be off in their own caucus — leaving the pair of us here. Two doesn't feel like the safest number in the world, does it?

Come out, come out, wherever you are — we might need some backup here!

That adolescent outburst probably begs some explanation. Is it that there was always the threat at least, no matter how big and grown up one got, no matter how smart, articulate — of being caught out on the street by the guys who didn't like the way one looked or walked or talked, who threatened, at least, one's self confidence, at most one's life?

Replacing a pair of eyeglasses could be expensive.

And only in my all-Native public schoolyard could I be sure the issue wasn't race.

Isn't that just the way life is? Aw, the innocence one preserves from one's childhood.

Or is it that it's still up for grabs who has the majority of teenage suicides, attempted and successful, gay or Native people?

Maybe I'm just mad at myself for being so easy. I was invited, I'm here. Where are all the other gays? I assume others were invited? No one else bit? So we're it by default, apparently elected the queers for the day.

You know there are people out there who actually write factually, academically, non-fictionally, philosophically, specifically on the subject or subjects around being gay.

Me? Well, I once got to do the PEN Benefit, had supper with June Callwood, remember her telling me I wrote "belles lettres." I wasn't sure at the time what she meant, but I was and am sufficiently shy and/or paranoid to think it sounded sort of dirty.

So I'm a rather queer queer to choose, if wanting to explore issues, social and political, around writing with any clarity was the intent. I don't write sociology or political analysis or creative documents.

I hope I can supply a bit of the — let's call it — emotional landscape.

Like from our panel's appearance today you'd think being gay were another issue of colour — lavender, presumably.

I mean, I remember trying to make friends with the out gay guys back in university — all white guys, of course, since there were no other Native guys there then. I was one of like about thirty Native people in the entire country attending university the year I started. The rest of them are nurses and lawyers now. Anyway, what I remember as most motivating those guys — gays we were back then, we hadn't renovated the word "queer" yet — what motivated those gays (beyond the lust that motivates most young men) was a mix of surprise, irritation and anger that their sexuality had disqualified them from privilege. God, they wanted it back. Suddenly, at puberty, somebody had changed the rules on them.

Privilege was something I have never presumed to, even in those moments in gay banter when one becomes queenly. And I guess I still don't presume to it emotionally. Having grown up on a reserve, I know what the rules are. I was taught to know my place.

Intellectually, morally, though, I am consumed by the possibility of justice, so I keep mixing it and them up, these issues of race and sexuality, in the stories I write.

Hey, maybe the uncoloured queers are off having a caucus of their own in the ghetto, or a closet, where they're dealing with the ways heterosexism and capitalism — oh, the whole hegemonic ball — are queering their privilege up. They won't play by your rules and have gone home, taking their balls with them. We hope to receive their game report at a later date.

In the meantime, we can have a little caucus of queer colour and not worry about representations. Can't we?

I mean, I would certainly like to assume to privilege — just enough so that, say, people would quit asking me when I'm going to write about something other than Indians — as if the centre of my world weren't worthy of even my own consideration, as if it wasn't as interesting, as human as whatever it is they have on their little minds. Consider that that assumption is what we in this part of the business, would describe as a racist one.

So.

The Race and Sexuality panel? Well, I remember that one of the other Native guys who attended it felt as out of place there as I'm feeling here. Not that he wasn't gay. Only that his community had not been so privileged as to be Christianized and so his liking guys wasn't the issue at home, at least. Sex hadn't been demonized, the body wasn't evil, the phrase for "Fuck you" in his language would only be an endearment, and he had nothing to complain about growing up there queer.

Yeah, we do need to complain about, say, "Christianism," if not Christianity.

The rest of us envied him — and were encouraged. Yes, the research — and anecdotes like his — is starting to come in. Many traditional Native societies, we are rediscovering, provided places for peculiar people. They had room to really allow self-expression, spiritual growth, nonconformity.

Could you call that socially democratic?

I bet there's a Mohawk proverb that translates "Variety is the spice of life."

Not everyone was meant to become a good consumer.

The image I've found useful, personally, and in my work and the one that's being useful again in Native communities, is that gay people are gifted with two spirits, male and female. As such, they are more whole, more centred, more balanced, ideal candidates for being shamans, priests, mediators between sides in any divide, material or spiritual, temporal or eternal, political or sexual.

They also made great babysitters. Something about not being saddled with the duties of being just a woman or man, allowing them to remember being children.

There is, if you're interested, a book called *The Zuni Man-Woman*, by Will Roscoe, about one such individual, We'wha, who served as ambassador for the Zuni people to the government of Grover Cleveland.

And Paula Gunn Allen from the Laguna Pueblo/Sioux in her book *The Sacred Hoop* suggests that central to the winning of the continent was the destruction of the feminine component and the harmony, the balance of male and female in Native American societies.

I grew up on the Six Nations Iroquois Reserve and we really don't think we're "matriarchal" — no matter how often anthropologists chant it. We think we're normal. But thanks for sharing.

My most recently produced play *The Indian Medicine Shows* was a piece that was mysterious to me as I wrote it, the proverbial compelling story. "Where's this coming from?" Only when I saw it whole did I realize it could serve in part as an illustration of the heterosexist nightmare Gunn Allen described, that we are so underprivileged to have become a part of. This small revelation was encouraging too.

So why would I want to write about something else? Whose soul is it anyways? That, for me, is the question, finally.

I mean, one of my memories of the first Writers' Union AGM I ever attended was of, one evening, being welcomed by some of the more senior members, to sit down and talk. And one of those guys expressed his enthusiasm for how the Union united us all. "Our differences" — and he pointed around our small circle and identified a gay man, an immigrant, a minister — himself — and me, the Indian — "our differences mean nothing here. We're all just writers." He talked about a tribe of writers — maybe he thought that would really make me feel at home. But that wasn't like any tribe I'd ever been a party to or heard tell of. It felt totalitarian, Big Brother, conformist.

He was quoting, I remember, some statement Margaret Lawrence had made. I tell you, it creeped me right out, being told that what made me an individual was worth nothing to the Union. Here I thought those differences between us were what mattered, that those differences were what made it interesting. Suddenly I felt like I was being bullied by the ghost of Margaret Lawrence. And none that night, in that small circle, disagreed with him.

And a lot of people have waved that Margaret Lawrence quote like a flag I could never bring myself to salute. So I've never been much interested in the Union because from most evidence its culture is a materialistic one, a guild only concerned till recently with the business of writing.

I think that's fair enough if writing is only about business. All those people who haven't joined, however grateful they might be for the practical work the Union does, are not going to see it as worth being a part of, if it means becoming one of the pod people.

And certainly from the evidence, most recently that of the motion in our package about "collective professional issues," materialism is how a lot of people want to define the writing that supposedly unites us. Because, as we are so often told these days, the spiritual — that's not the real world.

Which may be what "belles lettres" has come to mean.

We need to be good producers to supply the good consumers.

All this social, political stuff should be dealt with like sex in the privacy of our own homes. You don't want to spoil the romance.

I was invited, I'm out here.

I wonder if I would have felt more at home in the organization if that night I had not been taken for a token. Yeah, today I just may be making it worse.

Come out, come out, wherever you are! You, too, can be the queer for the day!

(1997)

THE LADY I SAW
YOU WITH LAST NIGHT

About Floyd Favel Starr's
Lady of Silences

Who is she, this "Lady of Silences"? And whatever is a lady, whoever she is, doing in a play about a bunch of Indians?

There is a sequence in T.S. Eliot's poem or prayer, "Ash Wednesday," where the bones of the poet sing of her and name her.

In that sequence — which was quoted in early drafts of this play, one facet of its inspiration — the Lady seemed to succinctly embody all of life's anguished contradictions ("Calm and distressed/ Torn and most whole") in a silent, final, English, Judaeo-Christian beauty ("The single Rose/ Is now the Garden/ Where all loves end").

It seemed to be an important part of the weird or mystic nature of that beauty, made from the Lady's contradictions, that it was neither quite cancellation or purity, that the consolation it offered was the vibrant, singing nothingness of white noise.

And the Lady was wearing white, though she was not the Virgin. The poem informed or reminded its auditor that Mary's colour is blue and that the Lady herself "honors the Virgin in meditation."

Perhaps our silent Lady was one of that virgin lady's sainted sisters, a contemplative in a sylvan retreat, or perhaps even Eve, the Mother of Us All, Eve of the Garden before the Fall, still worthy of all the praise a poet, or at least his bones, might chirp about her from his desert. A rose is definitely more than a rose in such landscapes.

But that was the lady on the night of Ash Wednesday in 1930.

Who is she, that holy nun or first woman, and what does Eliot's song of bones, his poem or prayer, become in the here and now of a play from First Nations Canada called *Lady of Silences* and in this final decade of the twentieth century? How do the song and the lady exist in the world of Floyd Favel Starr's play?

Only as allusions, immigrant glamour, whispers of a foreign song across Alberta and Saskatchewan, translated into, transformed by Cree?

The poem appears now only in Cree, imported to be one part of the ceremony of the play.

Does it still manage to be a song, a song in a desert? Yes, but since the desert here in this play is the Americas, or at least the Canadian prairies, after the Fall, after Columbus, the Lady of Silences becomes the embodiment ("Calm and distressed/ Torn and most whole"), if not the agent, of that event.

It is a weird but sure transformation, a magic act, the Lady into the pale Serpent of race.

She has become some sort of femme fatale full of Native America's anguished contradictions, an alma mater of its aching quietness.

It is no surprise then that in Floyd Favel Starr's *Lady of Silences*, this song in Cree is the song of bones the chorus of women characters, the three "Native females," the voiceless women of the streets, Ruth, Sheila and Lisa, give utterance to.

What better way could there be to introduce that relic of Whiteness, the dress Linda wore, to prelude the reenactment of that white girl's murder, and finally to escape that reenactment and exit the stage? What better way to reframe that murder as a sacrifice?

It is also no surprise that this song and its reprise are connected to the reprisal these silenced dark-visaged ladies took against the Lady of Silences who, through the person of Linda, was no longer their once-removed Nemesis, an unengagable absence, but their very present rival in love, their pale-faced sister.

Her presence as the Lady, that normal but strange fusion of the virgin and the mother, at the centre of the ceremony of the play demands from the dark women some contradiction, an imagining of other aspects of the nature and beauty of women. What erupts from their soured innocence, their lucklessness, their loneliness, goes beyond the song of bones into a speech of war uttered by Watatootis, the warrior woman, Our Lady of Noises.

This eruption of war into the world of the play, into the world of Native North America at the end of the twentieth century, is a thrilling if momentary revelation or admission, a breaking through of the great silence about the continuing war against Native people. Women like Watatootis might be sufficient to win at least a truce. Certainly she fills out the role call for any contingent of women.

And, of course, the admission of the continuing war allows the play at least, this war of words, this cultural conflict, to transform its murder again, this time into a justified killing.

These ladies have their say, and in so doing, lay this white succubus to rest, at least until the play's next performance.

How does the playing out of the murder of a white woman in a bar in a city on the Canadian prairie compare to the poet's cry to heaven?

This song of bones, especially transformed into the prairie wind of Cree, in this play that is largely in English, is even more of a mystery, is still, in large part, a prayer, a part of a ceremony, even an exorcism ritual, and this whitest of white ladies, this fairest of them all, is the body, the *corpus delicti* this particular ritual, this mystery play, addresses.

For this rich and strange mix Favel Starr and his friends turned to the inspiration of *The Blacks, a Clown Show* by Jean Genet. That play also plays out a ceremony that masks and then reveals and revels in a murder, a sacrifice.

That clown show also gave to our gentleman protagonist, Village, his name, and his aura of nostalgia for the lost simplicity of times past.

Does our gentleman antagonist and master of ceremonies, Detective Belmondo, derive his moniker and profession from some role of the French film star, Jean Paul Belmondo? Is this a playful way to make sure Canada's other founding empire is also given presence in the performance? Is that the message in Favel Starr's métissage?

In Genet's construction of *The Blacks*, he insists its performance is meant to take place before a white audience, imperial France in the flesh, and suggests that an effigy of a white person be given a place of honour in any theatre, any audience where no actual white auditor exists. *The Blacks* only makes sense when a white eye can observe the show's blacks playing both the rulers of white colonial governments and institutions — a queen, a bishop, the whole court scene — as well as the blacks those rulers rule, those blacks as the rulers imagine them. Its parody only works when all the roles can be seen reflecting each other's grotesqueries. Do these reflections also act to cancel each other out and leave us with the pale consolation of mere humanity?

No such white observing eye is present or called for in *Lady of Silences*. As much as it likes to be seen at the centre of every story, in Canada, an audience for the theatre or other ceremonies is hard enough to come by without getting picky about its makeup.

So in the world of this "Lady," that white eye is assumed to either be blind to or turned away from what goes on in the streets in the poor parts of town, what goes on in what it imagines as the vast empty wilderness of the country. Is that eye

blind because all it can see, all it is drawn to is the Lady over-
seas in her Garden, Belmondo in a film by Jean-Luc Godard?

That may be why these characters have been asked to appear
in this play, even so allusively, as bait for that white, wandering
eye, to give it something to fix on, to be nostalgic about, to see,
to help it take root or delight from this soil. That's better, isn't
it, than the proverbial poke in the orbit?

Or it may be that the Indians too, after so many generations
of being told that there's nothing worth their while in this country, also need to do a take or two of the presence of the Lady,
also long to look in the direction of the Detective's mystery. To
that desertified desire, this new dame Watatootis appears like
spring water.

Or could it be that mostly there are Indians in the audience,
that the eye is the one imagined under the visor-hand, jaun-
diced, bloodshot, and that the Lady and the mystery are here for
it to fix on in recognition?

Do we love her so much? That has to be partly true. Why else
does the I in Indian find myself laughing at the serious anguish
these folks, my folks, we, are going through?

But there is the laughter of delight, too.

Just listen to the music in the way these Indian characters
talk, mixing up languages, English and Cree, like habitués of a
multicultural street, like graduates of residential schools, with a
rich sense of the irony of high language, both secular and religious, used by low persons, with a sense of the anguish of low
persons with hopes higher than is healthy for them. The language becomes more whole and more holy. There is both surprise and thrills in the shift from vulgar language to the sweet-
est tenderness, from anger to romantic images that still have their
cutting edges, that are not quite worn to cliché. There is suspense
as we wait for the next shift, the next jab. There is possibility
sparkling like jewellery in the indeterminacy.

The ladies of the play wear it and thanks, perhaps, to Watatootis or teamwork (how else do you survive battle but with the help of your sister soldiers?), get away from their crime, the war, the play, at the end, and one longs to follow them off.

But Floyd Favel Starr keeps us, the audience (and himself?), with the two gentlemen of the play, if we dare call them that, and so we are not satisfied.

We stay with the boys, Village and Detective Belmondo, who are lost in the romantic shadows of the mystery story, longing without hope for loves of the past and for the truth of facts, their existence almost European. God does not answer the prayers of these Indians, he may well be dead, but in Village's vision, his lover Linda might well be sufficient, might be stepping out of the Bible, an angel; in Belmondo's vision, he is a wolf of rage, moving beyond his own darkness, beyond good and evil. Unfortunately, this new territory of freedom for both men also seems to be beyond humanity as well.

It is a vision of a particular secular hell we are left with, as well as the promise of the truth of our holy war where the Lady of Noises will be victorious.

(1997)

TRICKY RABBIT

About Beatrice Mosionier's
Night of the Trickster

How innocuous was the guise Nanabush, the Ojibwa trickster, chose for his first fleeting appearance in Beatrice Mosionier's play *Night of the Trickster*.

If one of the characters had not eventually mentioned his
name and reminded me of his reputation, I might have continued to be taken in by him, by what he was pretending to be for
the purposes of the play, a cute domesticated rabbit in a cage. I
might have ignored him and the possibilities he represents.

And I might have assumed that the struggles of the characters in the play to continue living a normal and loving life despite
traumatic pasts, despite the darkness of a long winter in Winnipeg, were simply their personal dilemmas, that they had nothing to do with, for instance, the anguished revelations of that
winter's Aboriginal Justice Inquiry.

But hearing his name reminded me that one of the possibilities he represents is that of healing, and that healing is something that comes both from the self and from outside the self,
from the community, even the world.

But Nanabush did not, while playing that part, look at all like
what I have imagined when reading or hearing of his adventures.
Those stories, which seemed to be about the time of the creation
of the world's spirits — human, animal, vegetable, mineral —
had put me in mind of a character who was a sort of adolescent
warrior, someone with more power than sense, a teenager in the

thrall of hormones or the newness, the strangeness, the beautiful weirdness of that world.

That sort of power, the kind of energy I'm thinking about, might be embodied — to create a contemporary instance — by a young Graham Greene behaving like the early Bugs Bunny. Although I know that Mister Greene is not Ojibwa (neither, I'm fairly sure, is Bugs), I do think it might be worth some consideration, if only to focus on the sort of characteristics usually associated with trickster energy. What if Nanabush's fabled misbehaviours were inspired by a delinquent Iroquois teenager wandering about in the wrong territories? But if that kid's energetic presence resulted in anything close to the myth, let alone the history, of the Confederacy, then the adjectives "Iroquois" and "cute" would not naturally arise together in the mind.

But *that* Nanabush was looking cute, perhaps even more so than usual, what with the contrast between his appearance and the unattractiveness of the content of *Night of the Trickster*. The play, after all, has in large part to do with the consequences of rape. Cute Nanabush was also mute, sitting there, in the production I saw, inside his wire cubical being fed the inevitable carrot by a young and pretty woman — Bugs and Graham would have been envious, if for different reasons.

Appropriately, as part of what his wordless cuteness seemed to be about, and perhaps also inevitably, the rabbit actor chosen for the part was white, the usual colour of domestication. In the context of *Night of the Trickster*, a play about a bunch of what the rapist refers to as "squaws," this innocuous appearance, the perfect bunny, seemed to me empty, spiritless, insufficient to the cause, a rather weak theatrical whimsy on the irreconcilable irony that white is also the ideal colour of sweetness, light, purity and racist power.

Where was Nanabush's magic in this unfair fairness? What kind of pale trick was this? How did pretending to be so reserved help or surprise anybody?

I was expecting and hoping for some sort of healing power. But Nanabush and the other characters in the play seemed to be just going along living out their everyday lives as if nothing much was wrong. And it almost did seem as if having jobs and roofs over their heads should protect them from their bad memories and the news. Couldn't they just ignore the pain? Would they not achieve normality by pretending everything was okay? Wouldn't the ache just some day go away?

No, it wasn't working, the memories seemed worse and there was more news — and that dumb bunny seemed as victimized, as powerless as everyone else in the play felt. Something had to give. So as far as I was concerned, cuteness wasn't cutting it. We were in the land of the bland here, nowhere near a place of spirits, of healing. Part of me wanted to say to that rabbit something like "Stand up and be a man!"

But next in that scene, in response to her friend Roz's rape, and maybe in response to Roz invoking the name Nanabush, the character Wendy starts remembering her Kookum, the sound of loons and a lake, a place of healing from abuse she herself had suffered at the hands of a priest. It was mysterious, magical, intriguing.

It was probably another guise of the proverbial carrot.

I suddenly felt confident enough to sit back and wait and see, felt that I didn't have to demand immediately that young warrior energy. Here, suddenly, was a different spirited energy at play, a glimmering lake. Dare I characterize it as a women's version of trickster energy? Where would it take me?

Back to something I had forgotten to take into account in the face of so much cuteness: that inevitable carrot and how common some of Freud's ideas about symbolism have become in our popular consciousness.

The next time it appears, the inevitable carrot is, at first, just part of the business of a scene. The women, Eileen, Wendy and Rachel, are, as usual, preparing vegetables for some sort of community feast. At the same time they're talking about finding more hands-on ways of dealing with rape, particularly since the Aboriginal Justice Inquiry has so charged the atmosphere of the city that the police feel themselves victimized. (Is it not disturbing how little criticism it takes to send the police into the depths of depression? It does seem like work needs to be done on building them a better emotional support system.) The cops are even less likely to help Native people than before.

Rachel, the play's central character, has been to this point haunted, even terrorized by the memory of her own rape. Now she stands, the carrot in one hand, a knife in the other, and reveals her decision to prepare herself to go out hunting rapists.

Eileen and Wendy are not enthusiastic about so radical a course. "What would we do if we did catch a rapist?" asks Eileen.

Rachel replies, "Castrate him!" and she chops the carrot in half viciously. "Make him suffer. Give him some long-term damage."

Ouch.

When Nanabush is not Nanabush, a carrot is no longer just a carrot.

I'm sure I winced as I laughed. I'm sure most of the other men in the audience did too. And we all probably, in unison, sat up straight with our knees together.

Did the women in the audience have a good laugh? Out of concern for carrots in general, I'm sure I wasn't paying them enough attention.

Yes, the scene that Beatrice Mosionier admits first came into her mind when thinking of writing this play about her experience of rape definitely did cut it, definitely played out an old joke that still worked. (May we all be able to say as much when we're as hoary.) There's something about essential differences that sometimes needs repeating.

Now we definitely were talking about trickster energy.

It was an admirable joke but part of me didn't like it at all. Perhaps it was too powerful, or tasteless, an image of a revenge right out of the depths of emotion, "an eye for an eye" with other body parts substituted. The impulse suggested circumventing our late twentieth-century system of justice in favour of a more mythically tribal one.

It just wasn't what I and most of the other men in the audience, I suspect, were up for. Most of the women weren't either, but for them just considering the possibility could be a perverse bit of fun, especially when a part of what the play is about is this dilemma. Most of us guys are usually not well connected to what goes on on the far side of that gender divide. So this joke does force us to, at least, face up, if only for a stinging moment, to the barest hint of what a visceral violation rape is.

It also suggests that the laws that are supposed to police rape have clearly not been made with women in mind.

In the context of a play about a faulty justice system, a system in which women, and Aboriginal women in particular, could count on rape investigations to feel like additional violations, that joke did get right to the rupture in the matter. I also had to admit that neither that ancient "eye for an eye" nor this modern version of justice could heal it.

But Beatrice Mosionier has placed this joke at precisely this point in the story for a reason. It permits the trickster energy to erupt and start transforming the play. What seemed a sociological drama with touches of humour shifts into what seems a social satire or comedy of manners.

Rachel carries out her idea, begins to prepare herself and her friends to go trolling for rapists. Her friends humour her, taking martial arts training — yes, Karate Indian Women Warriors! — and going on diets and trying to quit smoking. In the process, Rachel comes out of her isolation and pain and becomes part of her community.

She also is able to find the strength to face her husband Sam, to voice her fears about the peril their relationship is in, and forces him to make his own effort to cross the gender divide. Their dialogue is honest, ugly and funny all at once (Politician Sam complains, "I get screwed more by those guys in Ottawa than I do here").

It is this couple, their love, that Beatrice Mosionier places at the heart of her play. This relationship, that emotion, is what is at stake in the *Night of the Trickster*. The rapist had almost, wittingly or not, destroyed it. His act has forced Rachel and Sam to question their trust in one another.

It takes a dramatic sleight of hand to bring off this couple and their community together, a night full of the trickster energy of both sexes to restore that trust and heal the love. It also finishes transforming the play into a comedy.

And of course — we guys in the audience were especially thankful — it makes sure, after all is said and done, that carrots are, once again, just carrots.

(1997)

"ADAM" MEANS "RED MAN"

"Challenging racism in the arts?" I'm trying to say that with a question mark — although what I'm really feeling is exclamation. I mean it's not just the arts — it's the whole shifty culture we're living in and, really, doesn't that seem an insurmountable challenge?

The need to conquer any Everest is one I don't understand, would feel inadequate to and have no interest in.

It's such a weird culture.

I mean, for me as "the Indian on the panel" — or maybe I should say "the Native man" or "the Aboriginal Canadian?" I mean, who wants once more to pull out the whole earth map and point out where India actually is? It's old news. How about "the First Nations panelist?" "Aboriginally yours?"

Anyway, I mean for me, as who I am, a Delaware from the Six Nations lands in southern Ontario, according to both the laws of Canada and of the Delaware — although according to the Iroquois I should also be claiming relatives among the Tuscarora, nation number six — I mean for me, the first thing I do is, yes, start to take control over the names I'm called.

"Chief" is not an equivalent of "buddy" or "pal." And despite the ironic fact that I share the name "Daniel David Moses" with an elderly Jewish man who apparently lives in Miami and encourages by mail every Moses in the telephone books of North America to purchase an item called *The Book of Moseses* — apparently a genealogical resource — despite that fact, I insist that "Daniel David Moses" is my Indian name.

My parents, both card-carrying Indians, under the laws of Canada, gave it to me. The fact that my family has been Christian for generations is supposed to comfort you. All those Canadian laws that — let's say — discouraged so-called "superstitions and deviltry," all those laws and those schools and the reserves worked to the extent that I also even and/or only speak English.

A rose by any other name would be as red. Get over it.

Once my name is on straight, once I'm solidly centred in my own little world, my own tended garden, then like Adam I start to name other things. This can result in contradictions and ironies. Sometimes enough to make thought happen.

In my first-year humanities course at York University many moons ago, for instance, I was the only student in our tutorial who disagreed with the assumption that profit was an essential motive in human nature. "Not where I came from," I had to say, and the other students frowned. "Nor in many societies in history," the instructor grinned. It became my job to jar the rest of the class whenever I noticed them sleepwalking.

I got a good mark but sometimes, you know, I'd like to have dreams of my own. Do I always have to be part of the educating process?

Probably.

Well, if I can tell stories . . .

Stories are partly about teaching, no matter that I might want to think that all I care about is beauty. Beauty is a moral, human nature category after all, at least where I'm coming from.

I dare to operate on the assumption that a cultural expression that has a racist message, intent, assumption is not a work of art but one of propaganda.

I try not to be knee-jerk about it.

An obvious example: those moons ago at York, I sat quietly in film class while the instructor tried to separate the formal beauty of *The Triumph of the Will* from its Nazi content and have us consider it as a work of art. I sat there and — young and still too ignorant to argue — just got bored.

Art is also about being entertained. I'm entertained by the definition of art — I think it was — Picasso coined: "Art is the lie that reminds you of the truth."

But let's talk about a particular, probably unconsciously racist, cultural expression, in an effort to bring this some sort of focus.

There's a private museum in the tourist-trap part of Banff I visited the one time I got invited out to the playwrights' colony. It gave me the creeps. On display were stuffed examples of the local wildlife, eyes all staring as beadily as only taxidermy can achieve, posed along with and around mannequins, mostly faceless and showing signs of wear but wearing some of the most beautiful examples of Plains Nations' traditional clothing I had ever seen.

First Nations' works of beauty have invariably been put into museums beside other examples of conquered Nature. We're told it's because those works of beauty are crafts, not arts.

Some of my friends shrug at this vestige of colonial racism. "After seeing what passes for contemporary art in the AGO," they joke, "it's better to be associated with the other endangered species."

Of course, it would be even better to be allowed some of the privilege and power and patronage associated with having work in a place like the AGO.

And it's beginning to happen, although it's taken Native artists giving up most of their art practice to take up the practice of the curator. Controlling the naming of things is so important. If only the culture were a bit more careful, we wouldn't have to continually do this bitch-and-complain routine.

Still, it seems to be learning.

For a final example (this happened maybe five years back): I'm getting ready for bed and the phone rings. It's my friend Lenore Keeshig-Tobias.

It's about another Native movie no Native person got to write. They're going to show it soon on CBC. The promos have started airing across the country, images of conflict in residential schools.

They're even airing way up north where of a friend of Lenore's teaches. Her friend's worried because suddenly her Native students are using the epithet "dirty Indian" straight out of the promos against each other in the schoolyard.

It has never been heard that far north before. Civilization comes to the Northwest Territories.

Lenore says we've got to try to get them to stop this. We've got to phone around.

I agree to make a few calls in the morning, though I don't have much hope. I expect we'll be accused of trying to censor free speech.

So I hang up and go to bed and try to sleep but can't. My mind is turning over and over.

I have little or no faith that the programmers at the Mother Corp. will give a flying whatever . . .

I get up and sit down at my desk, get up and get down to work and the first draft of a poem pours out, poured out and left me able to sleep.

In the morning, I made the calls.

I don't remember but I think we were successful.

But I did get the poem as a keepsake. I'll end with it. It's called:

THE DOGS OF FREE SPEECH

I'd be glad to let sleeping dogs lie through their teeth in the sun, to let the bad breath they growl their dreams out with set off alarms in everyone.

My ears are anxious for questions to come from good peo-
ple who care about meat and how it gets got and what
master's voice it gives resonance to.

It's heavy, this wait for someone to weigh the words of
those dreams and part the ones made of love from those
made of hate from ones made of strangely sweet guilt.

What chance even my skull will get through? Isn't it
awful how sticks and stones break bones but words are
nothing, how the dogs guard their own even in sleep? Oh.

I too would sleep and dream on my fat but their bark is a
bite that keeps me awake. Oh I too would deeply forget
but I shake. Imagine that.

Imagine that the bones they chew are parts of you, that
you can hear each one break. How would you take being
chosen by teeth for the health of their dream?

(1998)

TRUTH OR FRICTION

Growing up on the Six Nations lands along the Grand River in southern Ontario and coming to some self-consciousness sometime in the late fifties, one of the things I knew about that self, about myself, and about my family, was that we were Indians.

One of the things I knew about the being-an-Indian thing by the way members of my family would shake their heads or roll their eyes or laugh or just walk out of the room was that the stories told about Indians on television were not true stories, at least from the point of view of our southern Ontario Iroquois community.

The only reason to pay any attention to those stories at all was that Jay Silverheels, the actor who played "Tonto, the Lone Ranger's faithful Indian companion," was a real Indian, the son of the Smith family who lived over on Sour Springs Road and who were old friends of my grandfather.

Seeing his face, a face we recognized whether or not we had actually made his acquaintance, made us glad and proud, even if those good emotions soon and quickly got obscured by the absurdity of whatever story Harry (his real name) and his masked sidekick found themselves acting out that week.

There's an old joke that must have risen out of that disappointment. It pictures the Lone Ranger realizing that he and Tonto are surrounded by hostile Indians. "What are we going to do?" the Masked Man asks. "What do you mean 'we,' white man?" says Tonto, and escapes.

Telling a Different Story is about learning the skills it takes to make our own escapes from the stories that don't tell our truths, whatever they may be. It's about having our own names, being recognized for who we are and being glad and proud about it. It's about our families nodding their heads, opening their eyes, laughing, and staying in the room with us. It's about sharing our escape plans with our friends.

(1998)

THE "OR" QUESTION

A Meditation

To be — and who to be — seems to be the question.

When I first began to attract attention as a writer — probably the year both my first published play *Coyote City* got nominated for the Governor General's Award and my second book of poetry, *The White Line*, was published, as a friend remarked: "Like a real book!" with benefit of a publicist — I also began to be faced with questions about what I can now identify as the issue of identity.

Until that time I don't think I'd ever really realized my identity was or could be at issue. I'd had a good upbringing, thanks to my parents, and my greatest struggle in life was also a luxury — the effort of learning to write well.

The question involving identity that seemed to be most commonly asked was: So are you a Native writer or a Canadian writer?

Hunh? Even now I don't entirely understand the question.

The reply I once made that I remember best — maybe because it seemed a small victory — was to answer the question with both an apology — I'm sorry. I don't usually think that way — and a request for clarification: Would my questioner inquire of, say, Margaret Atwood whether she was a WASP writer or a Canadian writer? I recall that my questioner did not — perhaps could not — answer me, that he or she went on to whatever his or her next question was, which made me feel, as I've said, a little bit of victory, or, at least, no longer puzzled and uncomfortable for being unable or unprepared to answer the question — because it is true that I didn't then, and don't usually now, think that way.

But just what is such a question getting at? Where is it coming from? And who really gives a Flying Walenda about the answer . . .

"But are you a Native writer or a Canadian writer?" Yeah, it persists. Some of you would even probably like to ask it.

When one's eyes don't glaze over, one is tempted to answer "yes."

But instead, I guess, I will try here for a moment or few to suss out just what this question is really demanding.

The "or" form of the question seems to assume that there's something of a contradiction between being a Native writer and a Canadian one — as if the two can't co-exist.

Hello? Why isn't flesh-and-blood evidence sufficient to clarify the cloudiness right out of the question? Hey, I've got both an Indian status card and a Canadian passport issued under the laws of this country. By these so-called real measures of the world, the question is meaningless.

But these sensible and legal realities aren't enough to dispel the assumptions — whatever they may be — that give the question its virtual life.

So I wonder if what we're dealing with here is a question of faith, not fact, of ideology, not experience.

So, does my Native existence question the belief in being Canadian?

Certainly, from my experience, my having a Canadian identity has not, cannot, make my Native one go away. It's something about the history of Canada and the way, for me at least, the two identities are very much — if I may coin a verb — "Métised."

Although certainly in that history, recently, Native people may have chosen not to talk about it, their Nativity — if I may mint again — for fear, as my dear departed schoolteacher lady Grandmother once warned, of "getting in trouble." There were, of course, laws against it, Nativity, a whole system administered by the Department of Indian Affairs dedicated to its eventual, well-managed demise.

The Department gave South Africa its inspiration for apartheid.

Hey, they didn't know what they were doing. Forgive them.

They were a credit to the Empire, the will of God and the Queen. Surely, they must have assumed, we can't really be committing genocide since our victims are already dying?

"The Vanishing Indian" was not the name of a magic act.

I'm sure the white man's burden was thought of as a sort of cultural euthanasia.

"We're doing you, like, a favour, man." The Good Indian is the dead Indian. "Onward Christian soldiers." And while we're at it, how about some beads for that beaver pelt, that woman, that land? (And more recently, that story.) "A dirty job but someone . . ."

Hey, they just didn't know what they were doing. If only they'd been able to imagine that we were human too.

I just can't imagine that, though.

I mean, look where they were coming from, where they were running from. The Dark Ages, feudalism, the Black Plague, the Inquisition — and they didn't bathe! It seems to me life in Europe was short and nasty before the potato arrived from the New World and opened the eyes of the Renaissance.

But lucky for us, all that history is almost passed, except for the poverty here, and destroyed families, and nightmare memories, and court cases.

History lives on.

But I mean, hey, we're trying to deal with it, (slowly, so damn slowly) in a reasonable and humane way without giving in to anger, although occasionally outrage does overwhelm us . . .

Which is, I guess, what the benefit of being a Native Canadian is about, yes?

I don't mind being Canadian. I mean, we haven't had a prime minister I thought it might be neat to meet since Pierre Trudeau.

But it's not so bad, is it?

How is it for you, oh un-hyphenated Canadian? Is it scary? Is that Canadian identity the worrying classes are always worrying to death now so fragile that my simultaneous Native identity somehow threatens to make your Canadianity null and void? Is that it?

Now that the white man's God is still dead and the churches have room enough to finally see and wave the *mea culpa* rag, what else do you have to believe in?

Does the question moan out of the blue fear of extinction?

Get real. Think of the numbers. It's not like we Indians are *les Québecois*. Native people are just not in a position to claim or imagine such power over anyone else's self-definition.

Hell, in the flood of information the media inundates us with, it's hard enough to hear ourselves think — let alone try to tell anybody else how they should behave like people in this so-called unreal country — if we can quote former Premier Bouchard.

But isn't any country only as real as the latest treaty?

I think, as Native people, we feel lucky the land is here for us. Without it, we'd really be in trouble.

And hell again, all we Native people really have on our side is something of a claim to humanity and justice and, as usual, in what passes for the real world the value, the power of that, is definitely up for grabs, debatable.

So why should my questioners imagine Canadianness is threatened by Nativity unless — unless they are the victims of some sort of delusion of powerlessness? Which, if true — if true! — might explain the nonplussed manner in which my "WASP or Canadian" version of the "or" question got dealt with.

No wonder, then, the "Native or Canadian" version arises.

And no wonder again, I guess, that I feel it almost like an accusation that by both being and declaring myself Native I am taking part somehow in un-Canadian activities.

But how else should I be behaving? I don't know any better.

How, how, how — at least in the context of the question — does a Canadian act? Like, good old Margaret Atwood? In some WASP-like manner?

Like, asking questions like the one I'm dealing with here?

Or like: "So where are you from, dear? No, I mean originally. You're not from here."

Is it unfair to say that in my experience that seems WASPish to me?

When, also from my experience, a Native person would say something like: "So where are you from? Who are your people? Oh yeah, I have a cousin —"

Yeah, no wonder my questioner was nonplussed.

The Native version does seem to be a question of "and" rather than "or," connective and inclusive rather than divisive and exclusionary, open to shading, colours, not just black and white.

When WASP culture is the simplified winter landscape we hurry across, and my Native background — I'm imagining a powwow sort of representation, something that will do well with the tourists — well, Nativity looks in contrast as fragrant and obvious as a smoke signal. (And I caution you I'm talking in metaphors here — the nicotine addicts itching to get out of the room have more actual experience with smoke signals than I do.)

What a quandary!

It means that if you stop to actually see culture, it can't be Canadian. You're not supposed to notice it.

Which is why all those Canadians fit in in Hollywood. When they remake *The Invisible Man*, it will star a white Canadian.

Margaret Atwood better be careful. She's so famous, she's becoming un-Canadian.

Excuse me. I've somehow or other rather erased Canadian identity. How rude of me.

And how unlikely, really. Look at the numbers.

But I did read somewhere that some universities in the States have started courses in white studies. And they're not talking Mozart, Leonardo and Shakespeare — high culture Europeans all — but tattoos and blue grass and surfing. So maybe hockey and curling and — dare I include? — poutine are Canadian culture.

Of course, among the categories I haven't talked about here is the one those examples beg, that of class — and whether or not Canadians have any.

Sorry. I meant to talk of economics, not style.

As in "Are you a poor writer or a Canadian writer?"

Hey, yet another "or" question both Canadians and Natives could answer "yes" to.

So, if you allow that Native people are human too, I might also start to talk in terms of any and all of the contemporary identity politics categories — gender, race, sexual orientation et cetera — but I've already used up most of my time.

What a mess you can get into when you don't watch how and why you're asking. All these mixed up categories.

So was the question coming out of a political context? A cultural context? A sociological context? An aesthetic one? A Canadian one? Or are you just happy to see me?

I think maybe, from now on, I will try to respond to the "or" question by simply, coyly saying, "It depends. Who wants to know?"

Because if my questioner also identifies themselves, I might be able to begin to answer the question in a way that just might make some sense to them in the context of who they are, political scientist, journalist, doctor, lawyer, chief of police . . . human being.

Yeah.

Any questions?

(1998)

POOR JUDD FRY AND I
About Oklahoma!

The other time I tried to watch Rogers and Hammerstein's *Oklahoma!* was on a black-and-white set. I only got twenty minutes into the film's two plus hours before the corny dialogue and the obviousness of the love story between the strutting cowboy and the complaining farmer's daughter overcame both my interest about what might make up a supposed "classic" of the American musical theatre and any pleasure in the familiar songs.

This time I'm protected by my trusty fast-forward button, a coloured set, and a vague hope that this "cowboy musical" might reveal something an Indian can identify with.

The colour helps. To use the film's vernacular, "It's real purty!" and makes things clearer. For instance, we're sure the lovers, Curly and Laurie, from their first duet, "A Surrey with a Fringe on the Top," will tie the knot before all the singing's done, though he teases and she gets cross, because their costumes are coordinated with the same colour.

On the other hand, even with the pause button, I detect no sign of Indians in this Technicolor version of that territory that in the un-reel world is often referred to as "Indian country." Could I claim the field of corn the hero rides his horse through, singing "Oh, What a Beautiful Morning" as evidence of aboriginal existence? But though the field looks familiar, the song claims "The corn is as high as an elephant's eye/ And it looks like it's climbing clear up to the sky," which doesn't sound like Indian corn, which is usually more rooted in the earth.

No, there are no Indians herein and even the cowboys are more like chorus boys than men, except for the swarthy hired hand, Judd Fry, whose lust for Laurie is the reason *Oklahoma!* can claim to have any story.

Judd doesn't rival Curly for Laurie's affections since he dresses in black, never sings and hardly dances. Is he in the wrong story! That's why Curly teasingly sings to him, "Why are you like this, Judd Fry?"

Our heroine so worries about the man that her afternoon nap yields a nightmare that totally, if temporarily, changes the realistic style of the film. In a Dali-esque ballet under a red sky among charcoal black fragments of a Wild West town, a bunch of prostitute dancers threaten the dancer versions of the couple with a sort of zombie cancan over which Judd presides like death.

Western story conventions often include violent men who do morally dirty jobs, like clearing the way by killing Indians, but they're never allowed to stay in civilization because of that very violence. They have to vanish with the Indians.

And that's what happens to *Oklahoma!*'s Judd. He fights Curly but dies on his own knife. And the community rushes, not quite comically, to a not guilty judgment of Curly so that the couple can head off on their honeymoon.

Judd's treatment seems unjust, unjustified, and mean. And I guess I can still, unfortunately, identify with that.

(1999)

THE TRICKSTER'S LAUGH

My Meeting with Tomson and Lenore

It's late winter or early spring, 1986, when I get my good idea.

I've worked part time then, supporting my poetry "habit," for a half-dozen years, in and around the city of Toronto, Ontario, Canada. I've been — here's the sort of soft irony a person with degrees in Fine Arts can expect — a security officer at the Art Gallery of Ontario. I've also been an assistant immigration officer at Pearson International Airport where, when I pointed out that harder irony — me, an Indian, doing that job five hundred years too late! — it was a joke not everyone appreciated.

In the meantime, I've met and worked with a circle of other First Nations writers — though I think the term "First Nation" hasn't yet come into parlance — a circle drawn around the writer/story teller Lenore Keeshig-Tobias.

And I've begun working with a board full of First Nation and other artists and community members who've answered a cry for help from Tomson Highway, the new Artistic Director of Native Earth Performing Arts, the Native actors' theatre. With him, at this time a fledgling playwright, we're saving the company from dissolution, transforming it into a theatre focused on writers.

So I've seen what we're all doing, that it's good and worthy of attention and, having seen another group of writers in the city getting attention just because they're a group, I decide we too should organize, and I invite my colleagues, Lenore and Tomson, to a meeting.

From the outside we may all look alike — there are family resemblances — but from the inside there are differences in cultural values, assumptions and behaviours that persist now as they did in "time immemorial" — some of our elders really dig that rhetoric — differences that persist despite the best bad efforts of the Canadian government and churches to establish their own cultural values, assumptions and behaviours among those they would know as "Indians."

So the question then is what can a meeting of a Cree musician and playwright (Tomson), an Ojibwa storyteller (Lenore), and a Delaware poet with Iroquoian roots (me) agree to agree on?

I'm sure we talk about ourselves, about our different journeys to the city, about the stories we're intent on telling and about our ways of telling them. These considerations, doubtlessly, include stories of our families and far-flung communities, stories which are still, years later, rarely told or heard in the city or any region of Canada other than those areas reserved for those of us who are officially "Indians." Yes, we grew up on reserves, more or less at the mercy of the Department of Indian Affairs and Catholic and Anglican mission churches: Tomson, probably more at the mercy, since he dealt with residential school; Lenore, less so since her talents took her to a private school on a scholarship; me, least of all at the mercy since I didn't have to leave home till I went to university. But even I am haunted by my grandmother warning: "What do you want to talk about all that Indian stuff for? It will only get you in trouble."

Whatever sense of our identities as First Nations people we've dared develop, we've done so on purpose, part of a first generation of Indians — that's a legal status in Canada — who've had the option of thinking of themselves as something like citizens. We were finally allowed the vote in 1960 without having to first give up our Indian status. It's not a franchise we adopt with enthusiasm; the larger society's cultural values, assumptions and behaviours seem so at odds with our own.

In our meeting we — Tomson, Lenore and I — must surely also be considering, if I'm remembering correctly Tomson's proclivities, beauty; if I know Lenore's focus, the lessons of our traditions; and, if I am consistent in my yearnings, the meaning of it all. We're finding, in our considerations, that we are at odds often but laughing almost always. We find, yes, we find we share a sense of humour that — we remark — we haven't usually been able to share with our non-Native peers.

Tomson is already at work on *The Rez Sisters*, a play that will make him famous in Canada, and the thread that weaves his story of a community of First Nations women together is a male character, a playful yet ominous spirit who embodies the hopes and fears of those women characters, a presence who is soon to be perceived as the first salvo in the campaign we're coming up with. (Lenore will use an Everyman/ white man/ lover sort of presence in her own work.)

What we're coming up with as our area of agreement is a rather rich irony. (The name comes in a laugh after the meeting as I cross the subway platform at Yonge and Bloor on my way home.) We come up with a political sounding literary/ cultural organization we call the Committee to Re-Establish the Trickster.

It seems, to us, that this bureaucratic convenience, this white washing "they all look alike" official government "Indian" label we're saddled with, is a stereotype. How seriously can you be taken as a human being or an artist if people think you're heroic or stoic or romantic or a problem? We want people besides ourselves to be dissatisfied with those stereotypes. We don't think they're doing any good. They certainly aren't doing us Native writers any good. You get tired of being told your work isn't credible because it doesn't conform to stereotypes. We're interested in getting a bit beyond the stereotypes. We want to try to tell something like the truth, in case somebody out there might be able to hear it. Truth is stranger than stereotypes, than ignorance, stranger even than fiction.

It's not like you can change the truth, take the strangeness out, at least in a democracy — and Canada is still tending generally, despite the momentum of capitalism, toward democracy. But why manage truth that way anyway? Variety would seem to be more than the proverbial spice. Especially in a market-driven democracy, it would seem the main course. So why not shift fiction more strangely toward the truth?

We are much younger then, but that's all we want: to open up a space for a little bit of the strange but true about us. (It helps — terrible irony — that the Oka crisis, that standoff between the Canadian military and a Mohawk community over a burial ground, occurs shortly after our own efforts commence, making them, for a time, a necessary part of what the liberal media frowns over.)

What we choose to lever open that space is a tool some anthropologist or ethnologist came up with — digging around through our stories, taking them apart, sorting those parts and slapping labels on, one of those labels being the category archetype, with a subheading "Trickster." It's in us to hope that if this Trickster character was strange enough to a scientist to be marked and re-marked upon, then it might also be true enough to get us all beyond the scientific attention span.

It also doesn't hurt that the Trickster as we know or rediscover him, as Coyote or Weesageechak or Nanabush, as Raven or Glooscap, is as shifty and shiftless, as horny and greedy, as lucky, as funny, as human as any of us. So we take that archetype up, start waving it around, the banner of our Committee to Re-Establish the Trickster. And for the next couple years, we do lectures and workshops to explain, even put out a couple issues of a little magazine dedicated to the idea that the Trickster is emblematic of our different worldview and the different literature connected to it.

And just what might some of those differences be, that this shifty Trickster entity seems emblematic of? Why take the funny seriously?

For me, it's something Lenore had said — probably in a writing circle discussion — about storytelling's usefulness from times immemorial always being threefold.

The first purpose, to entertain, is clear even within the context of the larger Canadian culture. The laughter of agreement that the Trickster provokes in entertaining us helps us to recognize the familiar, the funny/ ha-ha.

The second purpose of storytelling, to educate, is not quite as clear in the context I know, is a bit fuzzier, just because my mainstream peers — have they too been at the mercy of churches and schools? — fear being seen to be preaching or teaching because it too often means bad writing. The laughter that the Trickster provokes in teaching us helps us recognize the funny/strange.

The third purpose of storytelling, to heal, isn't clear to me at all at first. Writers aren't doctors, witch doctors even, are they?

But it feels so simple and right, maybe too obvious to need articulation, this entire tripartite artistic, meaningful imperative, and it occurs to me that nowhere in my education — and I've managed to attend two universities in pursuit of my writerly art and craft — nowhere there has there ever been consideration of the why of being an artist, only of the how, and there's never been interest in the who I am, a person from a specific community and culture, only in my talent. The customary first questions First Nations folks ask each other on meeting are still: Where are you from? Who are your parents? That customary other inquiry I met in school about what I did — they meant genre of writing, poetry or prose — is further along in the conversation, if asked at all.

When you come where I come from, not being asked that question about origins feels at first like not being acknowledged as human, like the questioner is rude or being cruel or doesn't know any better, or even as if he's imposing another set of cultural values, assumptions and behaviours. It takes some getting used to. A lot of First Nations people can't put up with it, don't adjust to the culture of, say, a university, and just make their way, unacknowledged, imposed upon, aching, back to their home reserves.

My colleagues and I had managed to put up with it in pursuit of our arts and crafts.

How? What was our strength?

If I can take as evidence this story of the three of us, Tomson, Lenore and I, meeting together that one time, laughing in both recognition and strangeness across our immemorial differences, I have to say that that's how the healing laughter of stories works.

The Trickster as we knew or rediscovered him, as Coyote or Weesageechak or Nanabush, as Raven or Glooscap, as ourselves, was so shifty and shiftless, so horny and greedy, so lucky, so funny, it almost didn't hurt us to be human.

(2000)

"A SYPHILITIC WESTERN"

Making The ... Medicine Shows

1.

"Where is this coming from?"

That's the question I had started asking myself, kept on asking myself, even though I had neither the time then nor, I admit now, the nerve to try for an answer.

"Where's this coming from?"

There I was, in the process of writing the first draft of a one-act play, a little drama that had begun with the title *The Moon and Dead Indians*, a mix of the poetic and the morbid that was from the start, without question, the right title. I was writing the play in its dramatic and chronological order, scene by scene, but I was doing the writing of each scene by hand, then having to pause to take my turn to type it up on the IBM Selectric I was sharing with the other writers in the common room.

"Where's this coming from?"

By the time I started asking myself this question, I had already completed the first two scenes of the play, was almost done the third. Those scenes had introduced me to the main elements of the piece: the simple setting, the porch and yard of a cabin perched high on barely arable land in the foothills of the mountains of New Mexico in the year 1878; the not unexpected characters, the inhabitants of the cabin, the anxious widow of a settler and her son, and their one visitor, a young cowboy. Each new scene appeared first in almost illegible inky scratches on the yellow pages of the newsprint-quality pad I had been supplied with. Then each scene reappeared clearly in courier font on the white eight-and-a-half by eleven sheets that inched out of the Selectric.

And I had been surprised and intrigued by the way a complex of dark emotions rose up through the play, and then surprised and appalled as those emotions got steadily darker. But could anyone have foreseen this piece that began with the widow, the mother, Ma, appearing like an insomniac ghost in the night in her bed-clothes on the porch, a rifle in her hands and the name of her son and a lullaby on her lips? I only knew it was right for the play that she called for Jonny and then for Jesus, that she sang one of the few hymns I still had in my head from my own childhood going to an Anglican mission church. And then when she coughed and fell into silence, into sleep there in the night, I knew it wasn't just a cold, I knew it was both T B, tuberculosis, the disease that had forced my own mother to spend the early years of her young married life away from my father in a sanatorium, yes, I knew — or rather momentarily suspected, because in the process of writing you don't take time for deep acknowledgment — I suspected that Ma's cough was both a symptom of that historical disease and a thread of what was just starting to go on in the play, a clue that other meanings of the old name for that disease, "consumption," helped me focus on.

And it was that focus on the disease, the *"disease"* of the scene, that kept me in contact with that little drama despite its darkness, the feelings of isolation, fear and hopelessness that first scene embodied, the mystery of what it all might mean, that kept me in contact long enough to meet the characters in the following scenes. The son, Jon, coming home with the dawn, efficiently starts to take care of his mother's physical needs like he's clearly done many times before. And because she seems to think his brusqueness is evidence of his shame at failing to bring her home a cure or comfort — he's been down to the town overnight in hopes of getting medicine from a travelling doctor's show — she tries to return his caring by speaking to his emotional needs. But why does he respond almost not at all to her comfort, her small talk, her teasing? And then why does he refuse to even listen to her fears?

Her fears. My metaphorical ears perk up, perversely or ironically, when I hear that what she fears are "sneaky" Indians. It's partly because it's nice to be mentioned, Indian that I am, partly because it's even better to have power, even if it is only the power to be fictionally frightful, and finally it's partly because this might be an opportunity to figure out just what this fictional fear that beats in the chest of every Western I've ever seen is really about.

But then the widow's fear is echoed by the sound of a gunshot and the play shifts to its next scene and in walks not an Indian, not "the sound of death" our widow was on about, but the young cowboy, the usual hero of the Western. And cowboy Billy looks and acts that part, with his "pretty" hands and his "How do you do on this beautiful blue morning?" manners. His presence, "a gun in the house," lightens the widow's mood, makes her feel young again, but it does nothing for her son. Jonny's mood darkens when cowboy Billy starts waving his "beaut" of a gun around, talking about "hunting" and "fresh meat." Billy also talks about the widow behind her back as "*la vieja*" and "*un loco*" who "will die soon enough."

In Jon's rejection of Billy's repeated suggestions, there's a secret, one that I, even as I write, am beginning to remember, is in part erotic. But as the scenes play out, I am also forced to admit that that secret also seems to be largely made up of a meanness, a cruelty, even an anger, which I, as I read it, want not to take any credit or blame for, which I have no sure memory or knowledge of. No, this sick, ugly mix of emotions, it can't be coming out of me.

2.

"Where is this coming from?"

There in Whitehorse, Yukon Territory, for the last week, a week probably in March, 1991, a guest of the Nakai Theatre Ensemble, a facilitator for their Writers Festival, I do remember now a part of the answer. In the last week, I've given a poetry reading, a workshop, and advice on and critiques of poetry to whoever asked for it. In the last week, I've been staying up late, drinking and talking in a smoke-filled cafe, and have slept in a sleeping bag on someone's hard, albeit carpeted, floor. At the end of exhausting days, along with the other writer/facilitators, I'm now fulfilling my contract by taking part in the final event of Nakai's Festival, a twenty-four hour playwrighting competition. I'd arrived intending to use the ordeal to work on one particular project I had in mind, but after the van picked me up to bring me over to the community college, when it turned to drive from my mountainside billet down into and through the town, I saw the last quarter of the moon fading into the early blue morning above the snow-covered mountains, and remembered another project I had long had in the line of projects in my mind as one worthy of investigation. It was a single scene in which a young cowboy, on the run after committing his first murder, stops to pass the time of day with the widow of a settler and her son. It's in the mountains in New Mexico, yes, the place and the time of the frontier. And the two young men talk in what seem deliberate banalities, as if it's the only way to ignore the craziness and the questions the woman keeps asking about the dangerous proximity of Indians. The moon over those Yukon mountains had brought that strange little scene, full of slightly warped clichés of the west, back to the front of my mind. And, of course, that last quarter moon was what had so immediately given me the play's title.

"Where is this coming from?"

I knew where that particular scene had come from. From a play I'd written about Billy the Kid — was it called *Billy the Kid Shoots for the Stars?* — a play I'd written for a workshop one year when I was enrolled at York University back in the early seventies, a play I'd written then with some intent of writing a history play and had afterward almost forgotten about, except for that one odd scene.

I once was asked about *The Indian Medicine Shows*, with apparent naiveté, by an arts journalist, why I'd want or choose to write about cowboys? "Isn't the Western a dead genre?" My reply had something to do with the idea that even a dead genre leaves telltale marks on reality or why else does history not tell the truth as I knew it growing up Indian? The myth of the frontier is a story of exploration and conquest. The way my folks remember it, however, it's a story of strange visitors who overstay their welcome and take over the longhouse. Indian that I am in this country, culturally, legally, and sometimes professionally, I had and still do have a strategic if not perpetual interest, thanks to what passes for North American history, American mythology, and even the imagery of children's games, in knowing something more like what the reality of cowboys was. I'm imagining that journalist might next have asked, "But then why Billy, Billy the Kid?" And now I can only wonder if maybe, back there at York in the early seventies, I had dared — undergraduate, working class (I grew up on a farm) Indian that I was — maybe I had dared feel that the upper class, educated shadow of Michael Ondaatje's already celebrated romance of Billy hid more than it revealed?

Or maybe I had already discovered my own alternate entrée to the story. One day, under the fluorescent lights of the library of the Department of Indian Affairs in Ottawa, I found it. I was there a lot those student years on my summer job. For the Education Branch of the Department, I was writing short book reviews, annotations for a bibliography of materials about Indians, a great job for an Indian intent on becoming a writer. So, one of those summers in that library, flipping through encyclopedias, maybe already researching that history play, I discovered what to me seemed a tasty tidbit. According to one source — certainly not one of interest to Ondaatje — Billy the Kid had probably died as the result of a quarrel with his lover, the Sheriff, Pat Garrett. Whoa, as we rarely say nowadays. Fancy that. I did more research, and although I found no other evidence in the historical documents then about the Kid's sexuality specifically, I did find further support in the situation for possibility of this sort of story. The historical West, at the edge of the civilized world of the time, was literally almost lawless, without established customs, elder statesmen or available women. And when you consider all the drinking, the violence, their class and their youth, it becomes hard to imagine how the heroes of our Western story would or could include among their manly virtues that of chastity. Then, if you also subtract a great part of our century's taboo against homosexuality because the new, at that time, science of psychology over in Europe had not quite got finished reinventing the Christian version of it yet, and suddenly every cowboy who cared more about his sidekick than his horse looks more like a kindred spirit than previously imagined.

So I go on to write an oddly tragic piece, odd partly because this history play, this Western, also turns out to be a clown play. That first Billy I write is a white-faced clown innocent, first an orphan and then a juvenile delinquent, searching for a replacement for the family the journey west destroys with disease, alcohol, violence, poverty, an innocent caught up in and finally destroyed by the New Mexico Territory's cattle wars. My odd little scene where he meets the widow and her son fits in here, that Billy seeing in that pair a family, a refuge, and not the widow's fearfulness. That first play is also odd because the sexuality in it is ironically or perversely chaste, a comic accident of a kiss the one action that Billy builds all his hopes on. For his friend Sheriff Pat, however, that kiss is a threat to his transformation from a wild and crazy gun for hire to a pillar of the community. Garrett sacrifices his relationship with Billy to consolidate his position. Finally, this odd little play lands well inside the typology of the Western — which may be how it wins an honourable mention in a playwrighting competition out of Queen's University. Or maybe it's mentioned because it's written in a concise and narratively forceful free verse, or maybe because it's imagined taking place in a blank page white playing space where stage blood can be spilled or writ as the tragic action progresses, a notion no stage manager concerned with running costs, I know now, would thank me for. But in clown plays you're allowed to make messes. When I get the news about the honour of the mention, I'm in Ottawa again, reviewing more books, and am surprised because I've forgotten I entered the contest. But the honour makes me take a second happy look over the play and it seems to me that, though I have managed to present a distillation of the historical facts adequately, theatrically, it is only that one scene we're concerned with here that holds any continuing human interest. Something about that woman and her craziness and fear of Indians intrigues me. It's a mystery I feel I can learn from, so I promise myself I'll return to it someday.

But not quite twenty years later, in Whitehorse, Yukon Territory, in keeping that promise to myself, I'm face to face with the craziness, the cruelty in the piece, and I don't feel like I'm learning anything. I had thought I knew these characters, archetypes of the myth of the American West, the widow, the good son, the handsome stranger, thought I knew them well enough to be comfortable with them, but I have never before really experienced this darkness. Maybe I've never before had to take the Western seriously, never quite believed it, always identifying with the Indians. My friend and director Mister Colin Taylor one day will typify *The Moon and Dead Indians* with justice and succinctness as "a syphilitic Western," but right now the only way I'm finding to distance myself from its darkness enough to keep writing is to answer my own persistent questioning with an occasional mock insouciant reply:

"Must be because it's my first play with white characters."

I was feeling then, needed to feel then, that the play didn't have much to do with me. I knew when I started on the piece that it was a Western and that meant that, by the conventions of that genre, there would be no fully realized human being Indians in the foreground of the story. But wasn't that part of the challenge for me, an Indian, to write about Cowboys, perhaps surprisingly, or with a bit of irony or even some political pleasure, claiming or reclaiming or just retelling a frontier story from my own other but human point of view? And wasn't I also just puzzled, having come to think about it, wanting to figure out what those settlers thought they were doing out there in the middle of what, for them, was nowhere? Just what were those characters running toward? Just why was the new life they saw ahead so much better than the old one left behind? And just what did they think about the mess they had gotten themselves into, Indians and all.

Yes, I knew from the get-go that the play was a foreground-free-of-Indians Western but had also realized that that wouldn't stop me from trying to see my own reflection in the background, because it's always nice to be mentioned. And, of course, the central character of the play, the mother, Ma Jones — an actual name I found at some point in my research — Ma does see that reflection. Yes, the woman's haunted by an idea of Indians as the cause of all her troubles — Where have we heard that one before? — Indians who lurk just beyond her line of sight, which is pretty much the line of the frontier. But, of course, I couldn't let the character Ma know it was really just the author, keeping his distance — mock objective? Ironic? — just over the horizon or, most likely, just offstage like the ghosts the play's title suggests. All in all it was a rich and strange position I found myself exploring.

And I had known when I started the play that as a Western, it would have to do with guns and violence and alcohol — I had done, as I said, my research. I suppose I had told myself I needed to see how that social complex — guns et cetera — fit into the heroic myth of the civilizing of the frontier, particularly now that I realized that myth didn't quite fit the social complex I knew of sexuality. Maybe I should simply say that I had wanted to get at a more real story of the settling of the West.

"Where is this coming from?"

I knew I was in real trouble when the gun, the Winchester rifle the first scene had introduced, the Western genre's promise of a conflict's climax, went off like a practical joke — the characters even laugh about it: "We were just fooling around" — before the play was even halfway done. Things could only get worse from there on in. Worse? Just what was bothering me? This was dramatic pay dirt. Part of it was — yes, it was silly to be having second thoughts in the process since I knew it was a Western going in — but part of what was bothering me was the high level of conflict in the piece. The combination of the unrelenting aggression under the charm and chat of the character Billy, without which, I admit, the play wouldn't go anywhere, with the almost equal resistance in the character Jon, together created the sort of emotionally ugly thing being civilized is supposed to mediate.

"Must be because it's my first play with white characters."

I know conflict in plays is, supposedly, a good thing. I knew it then because I'd heard it like a litany in school that conflict is essential for drama. "There's not enough conflict in this scene" would be a classroom critical refrain I, at first, didn't fully understand — and it took me a while to begin to. Maybe it was because, as an Indian, even one who's mostly Westernized — my family has been Christian since at least my great-grandfather's generation on my father's side; English, I must insist, is my "native language" — I still was finding that there were traditional values, if not customs, that gave me direction through life; and those values, I was beginning to suspect, were the source of my confusion. The pertinent example: I was brought up not giving in to, not giving value to, conflict. Yes, maybe it was because I'm the oldest child, maybe because I've always been big for my age and had nothing to prove, maybe because I'm just a wuss — or maybe it's because I'm Delaware and we were looked to as mediators. Never would I learn otherwise: I was a constant irritation to my high-school wrestling teacher, for example, who could never shame me into beating up smaller kids or get me to care about being beat down by bigger ones. And I still perceive engagement in conflict in life as dumb, as a symptom of a lack of imagination, of compassion, if not of humanity. The reason I persist in writing for the theatre, I occasionally think, is because every night it gathers an audience that embodies that valued harmonious community.

But imagine the discomfort I felt — I still remember it more than a quarter of a century later — when I was wanting to become a playwright, was a student hearing this stuff about conflict being of the essence. It felt like being told I had to lose my values as a human being to become an artist — which just didn't feel healthy to me. And no teacher could ever pay enough attention to know they should have been taking me by the shoulders and shaking: Hey, Kid, Life ain't Art, Art ain't Life. No, I just didn't understand that this particular "conflict" they were talking so blithely about in class — everybody else seemed to understand it without a doubt (I was the only Indian there) — was an aesthetic quality, one present, if you look for it, in any art. This conflict, yes, could very well be embodied, as it was in so many of those student plays, in a representation of the unhealthy relationships between psychologically realistic characters. What I didn't understand then was that that quality described as "conflict" could also be embodied in other parts of the play, like its ideas or story, or even in its form, its style. Who knew that there could even be plays whose very subject was a conflict about just what reality really is?

Before I continued writing, continued trying to be a writer, I needed to come up with my own idea about what that quality was, and I ended up somehow identifying it with what my undergraduate photography professor had called "contrast". Once I decided that what was of the essence for the drama I was interested in was a tension, a dramatic texture created by contrast, I got along quite nicely for years, thank you, with a minimum of that dreaded character to character conflict I found so unhealthy, so culturally incorrect, discomforting and distasteful, until that very moment in Whitehorse, Yukon, when I was caught up in the writing of *The Moon and Dead Indians*.

"Must be because this is my first play with white characters."

Over the next fourteen or so hours, those first three scenes were joined by five more, telling a story so strange to me in so many ways, I was, yes, talking to myself. "My gawd, this is sick!" By the time I typed The End on the last white sheet and handed the manuscript over to the contest facilitators, I had a first draft that was half the length of the final version and didn't yet contain all the historical details. It was also a first draft that didn't contain all the transitions necessary to make it playable, which is why, I told myself, it didn't even place in the contest. But that first draft already did contain all the necessary plot details, the characters, the emotions. It even included the waltz "The Blue Danube" because it was a piece of music I had chosen to learn during the years of my childhood when I was required to take piano lessons, as well as an abbreviated rendition of the ballad "Danny Boy" because, well, it's just nice to be mentioned. And I recall that some childish part of me goofed that "Danube" also referenced my name. I chose to describe that first draft accomplishment as "the emotional skeleton of the play," perhaps also because of the crime it uncovers, a solution to the play's conflict that both shocked and satisfied me. Even now I hesitate to talk about the concrete details of the murder of the effeminate Indian boy and the suicide of the mother. Even now I prefer to talk more abstractly.

Years later, when the final version of *The Moon and Dead Indians* did win a prize in a contest sponsored by, what was then, the New Play Centre in Vancouver, the director of the public reading there told me that, even silently reading the play, he had felt the unconscious working through it. By then, thanks to the prize, and just being wiser about its several origins, I was able to accept his remark as praise and not start talking about how afraid I'd been of the piece ever since it had been born a skeleton. Because I was afraid, that day in Whitehorse. I'd made plays before, had experienced the welling up of a story from wherever the work goes on within me without me having to worry too much about it. But always before, when that happened, I had been aware that I had prepared the way, done the research and thinking, sometimes for years, before the story was ready to be told, ready to unfold. And always before I had found I liked, even loved the characters in my plays. What scared me about this experience was not only that I didn't believe I'd prepared for it, that it did seem to me to be arriving not from my "unawares" but from out of nowhere, but also that these characters were as appalling to me as they were thrilling. That's also why I was talking to myself about the writing of that play, trying to explain it. Maybe, I said, it was because I was so exhausted after that overactive week, all my barriers, all the censors were down, letting all this come through and out or — who knows? It was as if I were afraid to take responsibility for the wounded, monstrous human beings the play presented. I couldn't have made them, could I? How could they be out of me, part of me? Oh maybe it was just the mountains, yes, that energy . . .

I really didn't or couldn't know then where that show had come from. It scared me so that when I got back home to Toronto, I put my little skeleton play away in a drawer with all the other undone projects and tried to forget about it.

3.

A couple years later. My director, the aforementioned Mister Taylor, phones to forcefully remind me that Cahoots Theatre Projects, the company that first brought us together to produce my play *Big Buck City*, is about to embark on a new script/play development program. I have been hesitant about taking advantage of the program because by this time I've become established as a playwright and think the opportunities are supposed to be for new artists. No, no, he says, this experimental project can only benefit from having one of your/our projects included in it. Colin usually knows the right thing to say. When we were first introduced, he charmed me and the play's producer by throwing words like "genius" and "masterpiece" around.

So although I don't think I have a project ready for public development, I agree to look and in my drawer I find, just waiting for such an opportunity, that skeleton of a play. Resurrection follows quickly over probably a period of months. Yes, *The Moon and Dead Indians* is accepted into the Cahoots program, and I find myself, despite the afore-detailed hesitations, now being encouraged, supported through revising it, researching, owning up to it. This process includes clarifying my version of Western speech patterns, a lyrical mix of manners and vulgarity, and deciding just where the phrases of Spanish will come into the dialogue. I decide that performing the whole of "Danny Boy" will not do the drama of the play any harm. (I also decide that the lyrics of the song, which were composed since the era the play represents — the tune's much older — as anachronisms also won't do any harm — I'm not writing history after all.) I find a definition of "psychopath" and become more understanding of, if not more comfortable with, the Billy character. This understanding includes the idea that, as a dramatic creation, he's someone a playwright has to love. There's a new book out about Billy the Kid and I use it for concrete details, although I hesitate to connect my Billy directly to the historical one. As the actor who plays him points out, my Billy is much better looking.

Beyond all the encouragement and the piece's now obvious strengths as a piece of theatre, what also helps me deal with "the horror, the horror," what helps me talk about it more abstractly and make sense of it, at least for my own purposes, are two related set of ideas I come across, probably months after the workshop itself. These ideas seem comforting to me, vaguely familiar. Maybe because it's just nice to be mentioned.

The first set are ideas in books by Walter L. Williams and Will Roscoe, anthropological studies entitled, respectively *The Spirit and the Flesh*, and *The Zuni Man-Woman*. These books detail the places in a variety of Native American traditional cultures of individuals who our western culture would have called names like "homosexual." In these Native traditions, which value individual spirits and their gathering to make a community, gays are seen as individuals who are gifted with both male and female spirits, "two-spirited". These "two spirits" could be seen as the resolution of the divide of the sexes and, therefore, representative of the value of the harmony these societies sought for their own balance and well-being. Because of this, these individuals could take on roles as medicine people, artists, caretakers of children and the elderly, and mediators. The book *The Zuni Man-Woman* is a biography of one two spirit who served as ambassador from his/her Nation to the American government. This set of ideas let me to see the play's murder victim, the effeminate Indian boy, as representative of yet another set of Native American traditions that have been repressed and almost destroyed. This allowed me to be sure that "sickness" in *The Moon and Dead Indians* is not limited to consumption.

I add to this certainty a second set of ideas from an essay by the Native scholar Paula Gunn Allen in her book *The Sacred Hoop*. Gunn Allen sees the meaning of the story of the settling of the west in an aboriginal and spiritual context, sees it as the detailing of the near lethal unbalancing of Native America through the destruction of its female principle. This allowed me to think of *The Moon and Dead Indians*, which tells of a murder of an effeminate boy and shows the suicide of a mother, as making sense, meaning something more to me than a dark horror show thrill. In the context of these sets of ideas, the play becomes a clear picture of the wounding Manifest Destiny did in progress, showing the tragedy of North America's history in miniature, and as such, is something I should have been able to take pride in. That should have been enough.

As I've indicated, the play emerging from the script development workshop went on to some success, first in a workshop production and then in a contest. It also created a bit of a buzz and was even offered a production before I had an opportunity to think about offering it around. The offer came from Native Earth Performing Arts, "Canada's premier First Nations professional theatre company," which had produced (at that time) two of my plays, my first, *Coyote City*, as well as the second production of *Almighty Voice and His Wife*, so it wasn't a surprise that their Artistic Director might have been watching what I was up to with another theatre company. I might have leapt on this opportunity except that that A.D. informed me that I wouldn't be able to have Colin Taylor as my director. The Native Earth Board had chosen that particular upcoming season to try to affect artistic development directly — something they rarely had done in the past — by strongly suggesting that a First Nations artist be hired on as a director. To that point in their progress, the company had usually hired established theatre professionals, favouring recognized talent over developing First Nations artists, at least in the visible positions, which meant, certainly, the position of director. In practice, this meant hiring mostly white artists. It would have been a sad political irony that the first established theatre professional this policy to develop and promote First Nations artists would have excluded would have been Colin Taylor, a black man. Even though I agreed with the company's larger policy, my own perception of my play was that it demanded an experienced director who was also a good reader, just the combination I already had in the person of Mister Taylor, the man who had read a skeleton of a play and seen the rich and weird flesh it could carry. I could not feel the same confidence in the alternative fledgling directors Native Earth's Artistic Director suggested. Loyalty, in this case, aligned with aesthetic judgment. The A.D. was surprised when I rejected his offer — Who says no to a production? — and I have to admit that part of me was equally nonplussed.

On the other hand, not having an immediate production was a relief. Now that I had or at least was developing a sense of what the play meant, I was hesitant to put it out there as it was, another tragic vision of the west, even if in this case, "my first play with white characters," it was the white characters and not the Indians who were suffering. The tragic west is a story I, as an Indian, feel like I've heard too many times before. Telling it again, even with this particular slant I'd discovered, just didn't quite feel like a healthy thing to do. On the other hand, spending all this time with a play just to put it back into the drawer it arose from also did not seem an option.

So where was this, this hesitation, coming from?

For a long time, I've had an argument with the idea of the tragedy, probably ever since I read a book about the Greek plays that suggested they were a conservative form politically as well as aesthetically. As I remember it, the book argued that the tragic emotion these plays evoke functions to immobilize the audience, to get them to accept life as it is, things as they are, to present problems as mysterious and immutable, at the whim of the gods. Tragedy asks questions of such apparent complexity, it expects no answers. From the initial stunned silence with which *The Moon and Dead Indians* was usually greeted — it took a couple of breaths before the audience could find their applause — it felt to me that my play was meeting this set of artistic/political definitions.

But I have always felt that this set of artistic/political definitions is something that needs to be got around. And I've done that getting around in other works, for instance in the play *Almighty Voice and His Wife*, where I found the conventions of the minstrel show were an aesthetic way out of the bind I had gotten into retelling a historical incident that ended badly. This getting around things is both an artistic and a cultural strategy. It's a way to express non-conservative values like transformation and growth, even though I, like so many of us, children of the Romantics perhaps, have a penchant for the ruined beauty of the tragic. It's also a way, certainly as illustrated by *Almighty Voice and His Wife*, of bringing into a conservative theatrical tradition that seems to value the tragic most highly, my own personal and/or traditional culture's valuing of the healing and the comic.

The audience not immobilized always asks the proverbial narrative question: But what happens next? I knew the character Billy, from the histories that had inspired him, was going off to his death at the guns of Pat Garrett. But what about Jon? Could he go on? How did he go on? Where did he go? I was slowly realizing that what I needed to do was write a play that would be a companion, a reply, and a sequel to the sad and solitary questions that *The Moon and Dead Indians* had asked. I needed to write a comedy to balance out the tragedy before I could feel like I'd written a complete work.

I remember this impulse was met with some impatience by Mister Taylor who thought we should be out taking advantage of the buzz. "You said what to Native Earth?" And what did I mean, the established, marketable title *The Moon and Dead Indians* would not be the name of the final two-part show? But he had, at that point, already joined the artistic team that was running Theatre Passe Muraille, one of whose spaces had been used to stage our workshop production, and so, after some further attempts at explaining myself and his realizing just how fixed this idea of mine already was, he started working to get Passe Muraille behind the development of what became Part Two of *The Indian Medicine Shows*.

I'm sure my first explanations of what I thought the *Angel of the Medicine Show* was about included phrases like "the return of the repressed" and "a comedy of western manners." I'm sure that I had realized that in addition to the character Jon, I would need to present the essences of the victims in the previous play, the two-spirited Indian and the mother, if I were to find a story that would be healing. And I knew that the action would take place in 1890, a dozen years after the first play, the year the American government had declared the frontier, that wound, officially closed. And as the history of the medicine show itself allowed, the two-spirited Indian could be someone I felt more familiar with than the offstage Apaches that had haunted *The Moon and Dead Indians*. *Angel of the Medicine Show* featured a Mohawk from Caughnawaga. And of course the mention of "Angie" in *The Moon and Dead Indians* really made me want to know just who that girl, now clearly a mother, was. She would also, of course, be my title, my central character, just as the mother had been in Part One. And then, of course, from my previous experience with the *Almighty Voice* play, I knew that the show part of the medicine show, the songs and repartee that stay far offstage in Part One, would have to have centre stage in Part Two.

My memory of the making of Part Two of *The Indian Medicine Shows* has no clear narrative. The process of creating it was the process of ideas first, emotion and actions second, making the actual writing difficult. Where Part One had resulted from, as my Vancouver director had suggested, "the unconscious working through the piece," Part Two required my conscious mind, weighed with ideas and new research, to sink into the depths of the anguish of the characters. This unpleasant submersion is much easier done when you have a story pulling you along. You can just blink in surprise and ask yourself, Where is this coming from? In the making of Part Two, I knew intellectually where I should be going but had to find ways of knowing and imagining the physical experience of my characters. I think I wrote the first scene of the play a dozen times before I could get deep enough to believe that my character had just escaped a lynching. The slapstick moments became a bit of a refuge as I felt myself finally begin to experience that drama. And, of course, the ambivalence of the ending of the play, the creation of what is clearly not a stable couple, thanks mostly to the unexpected pregnancy (not exactly a new story), was as close as I could get in this work to something like heal-ing, at least under that weight of ideas and history.

My explanation of the *Indian Medicine Shows* project even-tually came to include the following text, composed, I believe, for a grant application the theatre needed me to fill out. *The Moon and Dead Indians*, it read,

> . . . was a theatrically conservative but poetic exploration of the downside of the frontier. That downside was revealed as having much to do with the interwoven anguishes of alco-hol, violence, sex and racism, only made bearable by the play's conventional presentation. The play was described

both as wonderfully reminiscent of [Eugene] O'Neill and
as honestly unsettling.

Angel of the Medicine Show starts with the given of the tragic
emotion and activates it by focusing on the body. It is an intensely
physical play, a challenge for both the actors and the audience in
its presentation of literal blood, sweat and tears as the living and
traumatic result of conflicts, in this specific narrative those defined
by both the metaphorical and literal frontier.

The play blends conservative narrative theatrical conventions
with the vibrant, vulgar schtick of the medicine show to create an
almost surreal narrative that allows for both aesthetic and narrative outs, and real but unsteady reconciliations. It is in that sense
a comedy.

The process that got me to the point where I could describe
Angel of the Medicine Show that way took at least another year.
Then I got myself and Colin into a workshop for the script at the
1995 Page to Stage Festival at the Atelier of the National Arts
Centre in Ottawa. We had our workshop time with the actors at
the start of the festival, after which I retired to my hotel room to
write. While he socialized with the actors and other directors at
the event, I completed an entire new draft of the piece, a draft,
which I felt, completed the work, which satisfied my impulse,
which finally answered my question completely. I was finally sure
where it had all come from.

4.

And Mister Taylor, too, is satisfied, and so are the rest at
Theatre Passe Muraille. In the middle of a meal in the Epicure
Cafe with Susan Serran, the theatre's producer, Colin turns to me
and says, "Oh, by the way, I suppose I should have mentioned this
sooner, but, well, we're planning to do *The . . . Medicine Shows*

next season." Oh? After all that time, all that development, those years of coming back to that queer combination of characters and images, a production finally feels like exactly the way things are supposed to go. Although I'm delighted, know I'm lucky, I too manage to be cool about it, offhand, smiling, "Oh, good. Just talk to my agent."

Banuta Rubess, one of the other members of the Passe Muraille team, enthusiastically mentions the plays to the publisher Barry Callaghan, which is how I next find myself at my computer that fall, at the end of a long day doing a polish of the text, preparing it for publication even before it goes into production. I'm tired, losing my focus, so I shut the machine down, turn the television on to the educational channel, where a documentary about Carl Jung is in progress. They are explaining how Jung would interpret dreams and myths and give an example. Suddenly I remember exactly where the emotional knot that formed into *The Moon and Dead Indians* originated. In adolescence, one day in, say, 1963, the boy I then thought of as my best friend, a white boy named Billy, started a fight with me. How could I know then what I suppose now, that he was trying to prove his new and fragile masculinity? I was only puzzled and hurt and wouldn't fight back — I've already told you why — would only protect myself, which frustrated him. He wanted a fight. He left me flat on my back on the ground and walked away, muttering what exactly I don't remember, but let's admit to the process of fiction that memory is enough to imagine the words were "stupid fairy," which would not be anachronistic and would be right for this story.

In that moment of remembering, in the context of that example of Jungian dream analysis, I suddenly see that moment of adolescent anguish is the seed of the crime that was the morbid heart of *The Moon and Dead Indians*. I suddenly see that both the murderous character Jon and the effeminate Indian boy he victimizes at the behest of the Billy the Kid character are aspects of myself. *The Moon and Dead Indians* is, most simply, an early lesson about what I, in this post-feminist world, try to blithely refer to as "the hell of masculinity." But this is not a simple problem or one, I suspect, that concerns me alone. My *Angel of the Medicine Show* is a first attempt at contradicting that lesson. I'm still talking about it six years later. Clearly it's a lesson I haven't managed to forget, a wound so radical I haven't yet found a scar to cover it.

What this probably means, in practical terms, is that I will one day write plays about what happens next to the Indian character David Smoke and to the baby Angie will have, both of them, I'm sure, also aspects of myself and of what it means to try to be a balanced, healthy man or sissy or Indian in the new world that was created as a wound on the back of Turtle Island. *More Indian Medicine Shows* — a project that would please Mister Taylor. In the meantime, he — and I — will have to be satisfied that these existing plays have already begun answering the question of where it all comes from.

(2001)

ACKNOWLEDGEMENTS

"A Bridge Across Time, about Ben Cardinal's *Generic Warriors and No Name Indians*" appeared on pp. 6-7 of *CanPlay*, Volume 18, No. 5, September-October 2001.

"'Adam' Means 'Red Man'" was a talk given at Challenging Racism in the Arts, a forum at Metro Hall, 22 September 1998.

"'A Syphilitic Western': Making *The ... Medicine Shows*" was delivered at Dalhousie University, Halifax, Nova Scotia, 9 February 2001, as part of the MacKay Lecture Series "Healing in Human Contexts: Cultural Dimensions of Health" organized by the Faculty of Arts and Social Sciences. A version appeared on pp. 153-167, *(Ad)dressing Our Words, Aboriginal Perspectives on Aboriginal Literatures*, edited by Armand Garnet Ruffo, Theytus Books Limited, Penticton, BC, Canada, 2001.

"Flaming Nativity, about Billy Merasty's *Fireweed*," appeared on pp. 26-30, *Gatherings*, Volume XII, *The En'owkin Journal of First North American Peoples*, Fall 2001 and won the award for the Best Non-Fiction Piece published in that issue.

"How My Ghosts Got Pale Faces," an essay, appeared on pp. 118-147, in *Speaking for the Generations, Native Writers on Writing*, edited by Simon J. Ortiz, University of Arizona Press, 1998.

"The Lady I Saw You with Last Night, about Floyd Favel Starr's *Lady of Silences*" appeared on pp. 6-7 of *CanPlay*, Volume 18, No. 6, November-December 2001.

"Loving *Ceremony*" was a talk presented at the George R. Gardiner Museum of Ceramic Art, Royal Ontario Museum, 8 October 1996.

"Of The Essence, about Tomson Highway's *The Sage, the Dancer and the Fool*" appeared on pp. 6-7of *CanPlay*, Volume 18, No. 4, July-August 2001.

"The 'Or' Question, a Meditation" was presented at Brock University, March 17, 1998.

"Poor Judd Fry and I, about *Oklahoma!*, an essay," was published under the title "Where Are the Indians?" on page 40 of *Aboriginal Voices, A Native North American News Magazine*, May/June 1999, in a special issue focusing on *Oklahoma!*

"Queer for a Day, Writing the Status Queer: Reading Beyond Breeding" was a talk given at the Writer's Union of Canada AGM, 22-26 May 1997.

"Silence (?)(!)(.)" was given as part of a panel at the Annual General Meeting of the League of Canadian Poets and was included on pp. 39-43 of the *Living Archives of the Feminist Caucus of The League of Canadian Poets* in 1994 and on pp. 97-100 in *Siolence, Poets on Women, Violence and Silence*, edited by Susan McMaster, illustrated by Marie Elyse St. George and Heather Spears, Quarry Press Women's Books, Kingston, 1998.

"Spooky, an essay" appeared on pp. 5-6 of *What Magazine*, Issue 20, December 1989.

"Three Sisters, a Story About Writing and/or Telling" was delivered at the Spanish Canadian Studies Conference in Madrid, Spain, in March 1991, and at the International Association of University Professors of English Conference in Peterborough, Canada, in August 1992.

"The Trickster's Laugh: My Meeting with Tomson and Lenore" was presented at the Fifth International Writers' Symposium, Monterrey, Mexico, 21-24 September 2000 and published on pp. 107-111, *American Indian Quarterly*, Volume 28 Winter/Spring 2004, Numbers 1 & 2, Special Issue: *Empowerment through Literature*, edited by Daniel Heath Justice.

"Tricky Rabbit, about Beatrice Mosionier's *Night of the Trickster*," appeared on pp. 6-7 of *CanPlay*, Volume 19, No. 1, January-February 2002.

"Truth or Friction" introduced an anthology of student writing, a project of the Writers In Electronic Residence program, and appeared on p. 9 of *Telling a Different Story*, edited by Gillian McIntyre, Oakville Arts Council, Oakville, 1998.

"Words and Entropy, a Trickster-ish Memoir" was presented to the Department of English, University of Windsor, and to the Annual General Meeting of the Saskatchewan Writers Guild and appeared on pp. 16-20 of *Freelance*, Volume XXIV, Number 5, December/January 1994-95.